You Can Bank On It
Stories From An Accidental International Banker

By

Robert Sorrentino

Copyright © 2023, Robert Sorrentino

ALL RIGHTS RESERVED.
No part of this publication may be reproduced, stored in a retrieval system or transmitted in any form or by any means whatsoever, whether electronic, mechanical, magnetic recording, or photocopying, without the prior written approval of the Copyright holder or Publisher, excepting brief quotations for inclusion in book reviews.

Published by:

Janaway Publishing, Inc.
732 Kelsey Ct.
Santa Maria, California 93454
(805) 925-1952
www.janawaygenealogy.com

edited by: GreenOwlPress.com

2023

ISBN: 978-1-59641-476-1

Made in the United States of America

Dedication

Part of my daily routine for some thirty odd years was passing or viewing the World Trade Center. Both my wife and I lost friends on 9/11, and so I dedicate this book to the memory of the 2977 victims and their families, and to the first responders and other volunteers that have paid the price since this tragic day.

Table of Contents

Dedication v
Foreword ix
1 The Law Firm 1
2 The Draft Physical 9
3 Pepsi Cola 13
4 Wire Transfer 21
5 Due From Banks 27
6 Outgoing FedWire 33
7 Payments Automation 45
8 International Money Transfer 53
9 Chase Manhattan Bank ITEX 61
10 Chase Manhattan Bank Bournemouth 71
11 Wins 81
12 Tampa Move and Facilities 87
13 The World Trade Center 93
14 Money Transfer Investigations 97
15 Client Access Call Center 99
16 Client Access Acceptance Testing 103
17 The Eateries 109
18 Meeting the CEO's 117
The Sixty Second MBA 120
The History of JPMorgan Chase 121
Stories From Friends 122

Foreword

by

Paul Poco

With a unique blend of bold, no-nonsense approach to handling problems, along with incredibly simple and logical, yet effective, problem-solving skills, Bob has without a doubt left an indelible mark on many of his superiors, peers, and direct reports alike. In the pages that follow, it is abundantly evident to me just how much his style and stories helped shape my very own career, and my overall modus operandi - and I know I'm not alone!

So, whether you're looking to travel through the evolution of over four decades of banking systems and processes, which anyone in the industry would appreciate, or you simply want to take some notes on how to handle your business, both inside and outside of work, in an old school kind of way, read this book! Though the world around us has certainly changed during the span of Bob's career, his lessons are perpetually entertaining and unapologetically effective.

In closing, I would like to express my deepest gratitude to Bob for his mentorship and guidance over the years at JPMorgan. His impact on my career and management style cannot be overstated, and I am truly honored to have worked with him.

Chapter 1

The Law Firm

While I had some odd jobs in grammar school and high school, I considered my first real job as working at the MEJ law firm in Far Rockaway, Queens. At that time, I wanted to be a lawyer, maybe from watching Perry Mason on TV. In any event, I was lucky that one of my dad's best friends from his childhood was a Supreme Court Justice in New York State.

In July of 1969, I was clerking in a prestigious Queens law firm. Mr. J., as we all called him, was quite a character. I guess he was around sixty years old or so when I began and he was just a wonderful guy. If lawyers are meant to have bedside manners, I guess Mr. J missed that class. While he cared very deeply for his clients, he was always direct and pulled no punches. One thing I always remember him telling his clients was "Don't lie to me. I cannot defend you if you lie to me." That stuck with me for my entire professional life. I would never lie to my boss about anything, and that was a very good policy.

My early duties were pretty basic: go get the mail, put postage on the postage machine, do the filing. Eventually, I learned how to use the switchboard, which was an interesting piece of machinery in 1969. However, first thing every morning, Mr. J. would send me to the bakery for a well baked onion roll and coffee. Besides Mr. J., there were about five or six other attorneys. They all had their specialty: criminal law, landlord and tenant, negligence. But Mr. J. would do it all, so I had quite a bit of exposure, which was really great. On many occasions, Mr. J. would ask me, "So what are you doing today?"

"Er, gee I don't know."

"Okay, you come with me to court."

Usually, we would get to the car, and Mr. J. would hand me the keys to his huge Mercury and say, "We're going to Criminal Court in Kew Gardens. You drive." And he would sit back and smoke a cigar. So, there

I was, barely 18 and out of high school, chauffeuring one of the most well-known lawyers in Queens.

Walking down the halls, Mr. J. was always being approached by a well-wisher, former client, maybe a current client (re-arrested), or maybe a politician (he knew them all). One day we were walking down the corridor and a gentleman walked up to Mr. J. and said: "You cheated me."

"How? What?"

"You're charging me $850 for my case, and I went to another lawyer who is only charging $500."

Now, let me continue to set the scene. With this gentleman, were at least eight or nine of the men arrested with him, for gambling. Mr. J. said, "Okay, well you go use that other lawyer and pay $500, For the rest of you, it's $50 each, for a total of $800."

This guy's friends began laughing and mocking their friend as we started to walk away. And, it dawned on him what just happened.

"Wait Mr. J. Wait, I made a mistake."

We continued to walk down the corridor as everyone turned to watch.

"Too late. You're too late."

Mr. J. was a great man and was always fair, but it was a big mistake on this guy's part to accuse him of trying to charge too much.

Now, I am a big supporter of the police, but I have two interesting stories from my law clerk days.

Mr. J. told me many times that if I was ever stopped in Rockaway by the police, to tell them that I worked for him. Mr. J. was very good to the police and would give them deep discounts. So, one day he gave me some papers to deliver, way on the other side of Rockaway, at least ten miles or so. On the way back, on a road that was two directions for miles and miles, on the last block, a police car shot out in front of me and blocked my way.

I was thinking to myself that they must be looking for a mass murderer driving a car similar to mine. The first policeman got out and said, "You're driving down a one-way street."

"Well officer, I've been on this road for miles, and besides I don't see a sign."

"Look over there."

I did, and I saw that the sign was on the ground and let him know.

So he said, "Well look there."

On the other side of the road, it did say 'Do not enter,' but was very hard to see. I explained this and let him know that I worked for Mr. J.

He walked over to the other cop and said, "Do you want to write the ticket or should I?"

The other cop told him, "You do it."

Technically, I suppose the cop was within his rights, but as I stated, there were extenuating circumstances.

When I got back to the office, Mr. J. asked how it went, and I said, "Fine, except that I got a ticket."

So I explained what happened.

He asked, "Did you tell him you work for me?"

"Yes sir."

Well... Mr. J. told the switchboard operator, "Get me the captain!" He went on a rant, asking him why his people gave me an unjust ticket. The captain asked who wrote the ticket and said, "He's here, talk to him." After a bit of back and forth, Mr. J. hung up and said, "He said that you did not tell him that you worked for me."

"I did, as you told me."

"Okay, well we are going to plead not guilty."

Maybe a month went by and Mr. J. said, "Your case is on today. It's too bad you're not feeling well." And he proceeded to have the case postponed for a month. So another month went by and the case was on the calendar again.

"You're sick today," said the boss.

"Okay."

Now the third time the case came up, the police officer showed up in our lobby and saw me. "Hey, are you going to court today?"

"Er, I don't know."

All of a sudden, I heard Mr. J.

"Who's that?"

I said, "It's the police officer. He wants to know if I'm going to court."

The officer said, "Mr. J., I keep going to court and he doesn't show. I have to keep going to Long Island City, and I am on my way now."

"If you're going, he's not. But if you don't go, he's going."

"But, but Mr. J."

"You know you should not have given him the ticket."

"Okay okay, I'm not going."

"Good, then he is."

So off we went to court, and when the case was called, Mr. J. told the judge,

"Your honor, this is the third time the case is called and the police officer is not here. I request that the case be dismissed on the grounds the witness does not show up."

"Case dismissed."

Another incident was very strange indeed. Mr. J. would often send me to court to ask for a postponement if he was in another part of court or in another county. So, one time I had to ask for a postponement on a civil case in Queens. This court had a very slow elevator, so I would usually take the stairs. After I postponed the case, and as I am walking down the stairs, this guy came up to me and said, "You're just the guy I want to see."

I looked down and I saw that he had a gun in his belt!

"I hope you're a cop?"

"I am. Why?"

"You have a gun sticking out of your pants."

"Oh yeah, I forgot."

Anyway, he claimed that he just wanted to ask me why the case was postponed. But let me tell you, it was very intimidating. The whole story was that this guy had an accident with an older Italian gentleman that did not speak English very well. When the police showed up, they told the man to go home, and that they would take care of the whole thing. The next day, they arrested him for leaving the scene of an accident.

As it turned out, his son was an FBI agent. He showed up at the police station and asked to see the captain about his father's arrest. They said that it's none of his business, until he flashed his badge and said, "Maybe I'm looking for the guy who hit my father's car." Needless to say, they claimed it was all a misunderstanding.

While we are on the topic of misunderstanding, one day, one of the Supreme Court justices showed up in the office and wanted to know if Mr. J. was going to court, as he needed a ride. I was going, so Mr. J. told the judge I could give him a ride. By that time at least, I had a new Volvo sedan. So off we went. It was about a forty-five minute drive and the judge was asking all kinds of questions about school and things. I told the judge that we had a case before him. When we arrived, I went to park in the public lot and the judge told me to park in his private spot.

Now it gets interesting. I had to ask for a postponement on the case before him, and I went into my usual, "Mr. J. respectfully requests a postponement as he is in another part of court today."

"Are you an attorney?"

"No, Your Honor."

Do you know that it is a felony to impersonate an attorney in New York State?"

"Yes, Your Honor."

I think the conversation went on a bit longer. Anyway, a few days later I ran into my dad's justice friend and he was laughing. He said, "I heard Justice M. was going to lock you up." As it turned out, he was just having some fun at my expense. But I had no idea.

I mentioned traffic court earlier, and that was always entertaining, as people would have some great stories. One day they called a case, and the man had a number of tickets with fines over $250. Now, in 1970 that was a lot, even in New York City.

The man pleaded guilty and told the judge that he gave up his license. The judge listed off the fines and the man said, "I'm sorry. I can't afford that much."

"I see. You're sure you gave up your license?"

"Yes, Your Honor."

"Let me look again. Maybe I made a mistake. How's $150?"

"Your Honor, I don't have that much."

"You're not driving?"

"No sir. My son won't let me."

"How's $75?"

"I don't have that much."

"How much do you have?"

"I have $37.50, but I need $1.50 for the subway to get home."

"I'll try again. Hmmm, how's $35?"

"That's good."

"I knew I'd get him sooner or later!"

With that, the entire courtroom burst into laughter.

Mr. J. would often do favors for people, and take their tickets, and we would get them expedited. This one time he said to me, "Your judge is on the bench. You can go there and get them done and go home from there."

I went into the courtroom and sat right up front. Justice G. saw me there and adjourned the court, motioning for me to go to his chambers. So, I got there and a court officer stopped me. He asked where I was going. I told him the judge wanted to see me. He knocked on the door and announced me. Right away the judge asked, "How's your dad and what are you doing here?"

"Mr. J. sent me to have these tickets resolved."

Laughing, he said, "Okay, very good." And he instructed the court officer to put the adhesive backs on them so he could enter the fines.

The court officer said, "Come with me."

And the judge said, "I told you to go. Bob is staying with me. Bring them back when you're done."

Now this pissed the guy off. As the judge went through the tickets, he said, "Hey, these are yours. how's $2 each?"

After we were done, the judge told me to say hello to Mr. J. and my dad. When I got out to pay the fines, the PO'd court officer said to me, "You can't do that. You can't go back and see the judge."

Being a bit of a wise guy, I told him, "Let's go back and tell the judge that." We didn't.

One other fun traffic case was my brother's. He was in rehab at the time, and Mr J. was very impressed by this. He always offered to help in any way that he could. As it turned out, my brother had two moving violations that were never resolved and Mr J. said he would take care of it.

When the tickets were written, the officer made a mistake on the date. As we all sometimes do in January, he wrote down the previous year. Since my brother's license was issued after that date, it was impossible to give him the tickets. An understandable mistake, but nevertheless, legally he was in the right. Mr. J. met with the judge and explained everything, and how my brother was doing the right thing. The judge agreed to dismiss the tickets.

The case was called and Mr. J. bolted up to the

bar. He started to thank the judge for dismissing the tickets, and again how my brother was straightening out his life, etc., etc. The judge stopped and said,

"Mr. J., I appreciate everything that you are saying, but can I dismiss the case before you thank me?" (laughter from the court). So, the judge explained the legal situation and dismissed the case.

"Okay Mr. J., you can thank me now." More laughter, and true to form, Mr. J. did another thank you.

Just to show you how great a guy Mr. J. was, I had told him that my brother was out of rehab and working at Barney's. One day we were in lower Manhattan and he asked me if my brother was working that day. I told him that I thought that he was, and he said, "Let's go."

"To Barney's?" I asked.

"Yes."

When we got there, he told me that he wanted to buy me a suit, so that my brother could make the commission on the sale. He was like that with everything; a very generous man. He would often tell me to go through the courthouse, find our lawyers, and tell them that we were all going to the Pastrami King for lunch.

One last funny office story was when a client came into the office and Mr. J. told me to go get his file.

"What's his name?"

"If I knew his name, I wouldn't have asked you to get his file."

So, I had to go into every attorney's office to have them look in the lobby and see if they knew who the client was. Luckily, one of them knew who he was, and I was able to get the file.

All of the attorneys there were wonderful guys and treated me as a colleague. Even though I didn't go on to law school, this was a great experience. And I loved every minute.

Chapter 2

The Draft Physical

In the summer of 1971, I left the law firm, under dubious circumstances, which I would rather not discuss. And I also finished two years of community college. Not long after, I received my notice of 1-A draft classification and was ordered to report to Fort Hamilton in Brooklyn for my physical.

For about a year or so, I had this lump in my groin, that mostly didn't bother me. But since I had to go for my physical, I figured I would have this looked at. So I went to the family doctor in Whitestone, Dr. Cohen, He told me that I have a hernia, and that his son, a surgeon at Parson's Hospital, could repair it the following week. So I told him, "No, I have the draft physical in two weeks and I need to have that with me when I go." He laughed and said "Okay, we'll do it after the physical."

Now, Fort Hamilton was a scene straight out of Arlo Gutherie's "Alice's Restaurant," sans the father stabbers, mother rapers, and father rapers on the "Group W" bench.

First thing, we stripped down to our underwear, and they gave us a bag to carry all of our belongings around. Now there are guys carrying around huge envelopes with their x-rays, medical records, etc. Me, I just had my hernia.

The first station is the urine test. They handed us a glass and we went into a room with maybe 100 guys. We had to pee in the cup and bring it over to a chest high station with a few sergeants. So, this one guy went up to the desk and purposely tipped his cup, so the pee went all over the desk. Needless to say, the sergeants were not happy. They gave the kid another cup and told him he was not leaving until he filled it. He shouted out, "I need some piss!" Several of us obliged and within a minute he was back at the desk with a cup filled to the brim. The sergeants were perplexed to say the least.

We wound around the complex for several hours stopping at all the various stations. At the weigh-in, we had to be above or below a certain weight. Now, I didn't know the minimum, but the maximum was 300 pounds. I know this because one guy tipped the scale at 301 1/2 pounds.

The corpsman told him, "You're one and a half pounds overweight. I can mark it down and you can come back in a few weeks to see if you are under three hundred." The guy said, "Are you kidding me? I've been eating for two weeks straight to get over three hundred!"

I've gotten used to giving blood by now, but back in the day it scared the crap out of me. So then, I was shaking in my boots, waiting for my turn. I got up to the corpsman and he said, "It's going to be easier if you stop shaking." Not to mention, there was no sitting down, you just stood there. Well, I got through it and he handed me three glass vials of warm blood, and told me to bring it over there. I was holding on to those babies for dear life, because I knew that if I dropped them, I would have to start over.

I made it through the eye test, the hearing test, and I think there was also some sort of mental test. Finally, after three hours, I got to the doctor that gives you the physical exam. "Turn your head and cough."

"You have a hernia."

"Yes, I know."

"Ok you have to go through that doorway and see the major."

Eventually, I got called into a little cubicle where a major was sitting. "You know that you have a hernia?"

"Yes."

"How do you know that?"

"Well, my doctor told me last week, and your doctor told me ten minutes ago."

Apparently, he didn't like that answer. He proceeded to yell at me about how his doctor was not supposed to tell me anything, and that I had to get the information from him, and on and on.

I said, "Hey pal, don't yell at me. Go yell at him." Needless to say, he didn't like that response. Finally, he jumped up and yelled, "What side is it on?!"

"The right." He proceeded to spend a few minutes explaining that I was unfit for military service at that time, what my new classification was, that I could be called back, and so forth.

"That's the best news I've heard all day. Can I go now?"

"Get out!"

Now you think this is the end of the story. But as I headed out of the building, I got stopped by a corporal. "Where are you going?"

"Home. The major told me to leave."

"You can't leave yet. You didn't have lunch." It was only 11 a.m.

"Can't I have lunch at home?"

"Yes, but you have to sign a paper stating that you were offered lunch and refused."

I signed and went on my merry way.

My family was lucky in that I only had one cousin that went to Vietnam. When he arrived, they asked if anyone knew how to cook. He didn't, but he raised his hand anyway. Luckily, he didn't get in trouble when they asked why he said he could cook. He told them it was better than getting shot at in the jungle. He spent his tour in the officer's mess in Saigon. Later, he opened restaurants in NYC and Long Island.

My ex-wife's brother was very lucky. The normal tour in Vietnam at the time was thirteen months. When he had less than that, we all assumed he would not have to go. But with about ten months left, he was sent over. He had applied for a technical college in the states and was accepted, but he still had a month left in the service. He applied and was granted an early out. A week after he left Vietnam, the jeep that he and his mates would ride in on a daily basis hit a mine, and they were all KIA. Very sad story.

One of my good friends was wounded there, came back to the US, and became a police officer. He was wounded in NYC when he responded to a robbery in progress call. He was hit in the leg, but later they found a bullet hole in his hat that just missed hitting him.

Chapter 3
Pepsi Cola

A few months after getting laid off from the law firm, my surgery, and fun at Fort Hamilton, my cousin Frank called and told me that he had an opening loading trucks at Pepsi Cola in Brooklyn. Frank was the second in command at the warehouse, and he was only about 28 years old. If I was interested, I should go to the union hall on 14th street in NYC on Saturday and tell them that he sent me for the job. Apparently, at that time, the Teamsters Union was doing the hiring.

I went down there and I think I went up a flight of stairs and entered this wood paneled room with some benches. I looked around and I saw a sort of speakeasy window and a doorbell. I rung the bell and a little door opened.

"Who are you, what do you want?" said the man.

"Bob Sorrentino. My cousin, Frank Nicoletti, sent me for the job opening at Pepsi."

"I saw him yesterday. He didn't tell me. Do you have his number?"

"I don't."

"I have it. Wait there."

A few minutes went by and the people door opened. This guy was all smiles as he ushered me into a massive office, with a bar.

"Come on in, Frank says you're a good kid. That's what we like, good Italian boys. You know Pepsi wants to hire their people, then they want me to deal with the problems. We're not going to have any problems with a good Italian boy?"

"No."

"Of course not. You need to go to Long Island City for a physical. When can you go, Monday? But it's ok, that will all be fine. You can start right after that. You tell Frank, everything is good."

I think I started the following Monday after the physical. So, the warehouse was on Ave. D, and not too far from one of the worst areas in Brooklyn. But it only took me about 30 minutes from my home in Flushing. My hours were from 5 p.m. to 2 a.m. Monday to Friday, and I made $5 per hour. Now that may not seem like much, but $200 a week in 1971, at the age of 20, man I was rolling in dough. Also, we got time and a half after eight hours and double time after 10 hours,]. Some weeks in the summer I would make over $300. And we got paid cash weekly on Friday at 9 p.m.

When you started, your first job was on the "shit pile." That was the place where the loaders would drop off the pallets pulled from a truck that had less than 36 cases for bottles, or 88 for cans. You would then have to build up a new pallet from the ones dropped off, based on what the loader needed. For example, the loader might drop off a pallet of 10 and say, "Make this 30." I had to build that up from the other pallets dropped off. I have to say that the black guys were the best. They would get off their forklift and help. They would also grab the empty pallets and help stack them. The white guys, with the exception of one or two, sucked. I learned a real valuable lesson that helped as a supervisor and manager later in my career.

After a few weeks, I was told that I could start practicing with the forklift after lunch and during breaks. It wasn't too difficult to learn and I at least had some independence on the "shit-pile." I don't remember exactly when I was moved to loading, but it wasn't that long. I think we loaded about 94 trucks every night. And I guess we had about 12 or 14 loaders, and two men, who would rotate the trucks that needed to be loaded from the parking area to the warehouse. The warehouse also did bottling for Pepsi. But the cans and other flavors were brought in by an 18-wheeler.

I got very proficient at loading and would average eight trucks a night. That didn't sit well with many of the men, as they thought I was working too hard. I would tell them that my night went quicker when I was working, as opposed to sitting on the can! Anyway, some thought I was a spy, as they learned that Frank was my cousin. That all changed one hot summer night.

As I said earlier, I loaded the most trucks per night. One night, when it was probably well over 100 degrees in the warehouse, and I just completed my eighth truck, I grabbed a Pepsi and parked my forklift in the yard to get some air. Joe, the assistant foreman, came out and told me that it was only 1:30, (we actually would finish at 1:45, as we were given 15 minutes wash up time), and sent me to the room with all the broken cases and loose bottles to straighten it up.

I didn't say anything, and I did as he asked. But I was pretty pissed off.

The system worked as follows: At 5 p.m. we would line up by the foreman and he would hand us a ticket that had the truck number and the driver's order. When we completed that truck, we would hand it in and be assigned a new truck. I got my first truck and it took four hours to finish. Just before lunch, I handed in the ticket.

Joe said, "What's going on? You only loaded one truck."

"I'm not feeling well. I should probably go home." According to union rules, because there wasn't a nurse on duty, they could not stop someone from leaving if they said that they were sick. So I loaded one more truck after lunch, and by the end of the night there were six trucks left to load. As I handed in my second ticket, Joe wanted to know if I was working overtime. "Nope, I'm sick." Normally, everyone would jump on the overtime. With six trucks, it was an easy four hours of pay. But, because they knew I was sticking it to Joe, coupled with the fact that many did not like him to begin with, everyone was refusing, except for the two worst loaders... LOL!

Those two guys took seven and a half hours, until 9:30 a.m. to finish. The drivers were pissed as it was summer and they had full loads. They wanted to be out by 6 or 7 a.m.

Typically, I would not see my cousin. But that day, he must have been waiting, because when I showed up, he was cracking up.

"What the fuck did you do to Joe last night?"

"I didn't do anything. He treated me like shit the night before, and I had to teach him a lesson." Mind you, Joe was a WWII army vet.

"He's pissed off at you."

"He'll get over it."

That night, just for spite, or to be a wise guy, probably the latter, I went out and repeated the process from two nights before. I finished my eight trucks, got a Pepsi, and relaxed in the yard at 1:30.

Joe walked out, saw me, turned around, and walked away without a word. The following week I handed him a ticket and he said, "You're a real smart ass."

"How so?"

"You weren't sick the other night."

"You're right, but I'm your best loader and you stuck me in the crap. You want me to help someone load a truck fine, put the lazy guys in there, not me!"

We never had another issue.

The warehouse had a back entrance from the parking lot, and a front entrance to the street. The trucks would come in from the back and park for us to load. The shifters would keep them moving through the process. One day we saw a truck pulling out of the front, and the two shifters walking from the back door. The foreman looked at the truck, then at the shifters, then at the truck. He realized that someone was stealing a truck filled with soda and started to chase the truck out the door. He never caught up, and they found the truck a few days later in a bad part of Brooklyn. Emptied out, of course.

We had some real characters in that place. One guy was a stoned-out heroin junkie. Some-how he had the newest and best forklift. After lunch, we would see him nodding out as he drove through the warehouse.

"WHITEY, WAKE UP!" It's amazing no one got run over.

We had another big Polish guy who went by the nickname of "Money," as he was very cheap. Money ran his own coffee concession in the break room, where for the most part he "appropriated" most of the supplies.

His typical MO was to collect any cups, stirrers, sugar napkins, and cream from outside coffee runs for his business. When we went into double overtime, the bosses would let one of us go for a coffee run to the local diner. We would collect the orders and go pick it up. One night when it was my turn, Money started collecting all the leftover stuff.

I asked, "What are you doing?"

"Collecting my stuff."

"How is it yours? I went and got it, so it must be mine."

"It's always mine."

"Who says?"

Anyway, we went 'round and 'round on this for quite some time, until he finally gave up and walked away. Rumor had it that "Money" did some time for manslaughter. Arguing this point with him was probably not very wise.

Another unwise thing I did was when a police car pulled into the warehouse for some soda. The boss told me to go get two cases of Pepsi and two cases of oranges. So, I went and got them, and got back to the car where the trunk was open, and I sat. The cop asked if I was going to help, and I said no. He then asked me to lift up the forks so he doesn't have to bend down and I said, "No, I have to pay for this shit and you're getting it for free. The least you can do is work for it." Needless to say, he was not happy and my boss freaked out on me. Rightfully so.

I don't recall anyone ever getting seriously hurt, but there were some close calls. The soda would come off the line cold, and then put into cardboard boxes. In the summer, because of the heat in the warehouse, the soda would sweat, the boxes would get wet, and start to collapse. Then, we would have an avalanche of Pepsi coming at us. Many times it would block the warehouse floor so the trucks could not move. That was always good for a couple of hours overtime while we cleared the way.

The forks could reach, I guess twenty to twenty-five mph. It doesn't sound like much, but we were in an enclosed building with narrow lanes of passage. Once, I had thirty-six cases of sixteen-ounce bottles (plastic was not yet the thing), and I spun the wheel to make a turn right by the foreman. I was going too fast. The forklift spun, but the soda didn't, and came crashing down right by his feet. Luckily, he was not hurt.

The pallets of cans were stacked 11 cases high to a pallet and three pallets high. So maybe between 16 to 20 feet high. The pallets were shorter than the forks. So we had to be very careful when trying to grab the top pallet, to be sure that we didn't hook the one behind it. One day, a new loader hooked the back pallet and a couple of hundred cases came crashing down around him.

We had two Bobs there. I was white Bob, and we had another guy who was black Bob. We became good friends and occasionally I would give him a ride home, which was in one of the roughest black neighborhoods in Brooklyn. One day he asked if I was hungry and I said, "Sure." So we went into the White Castle, and the whole place turned and looked at me. Now mind you, it's like 2:30 in the morning, and me and the castle are the only two white things there. Black Bob started cracking up. "You're with me, brother. No one's going to bother you."

Another time, after dropping him off, I headed back to the highway along a road with a traffic light on every corner. Back then, there was no amber, just red and green. Again, it's about 2:30 in the morning and as the lights were turning red, I just drove through them. About halfway, I spied flashing lights behind me, and I stopped. The car had two cops, one white and one black.

The white cop comes over to my car.

"You know you went through a red light?"

"Yes officer. I went through several." "Why?" "Do you think I'm going to stop at a red light in this neighborhood at 2:30 in the morning?"

"Well why are you here in the first place?"

I explained that I worked at Pepsi on Ave. D, and that I dropped off a co-worker, and was on my way back to the highway. So he said, "Well, we didn't really stop you for the lights. We figure if we see a young white guy in the area this early in the morning, he's buying drugs." Luckily, I had my Pepsi uniform on, and he was really nice about it.

"Do me a favor."

"What's that?"

"When you're running the lights, just be sure no one is coming the other way."

I saw him get back in the car and they both cracked up.

My ex-wife and I had friends that lived in Ridgewood Queens, and she was visiting them. I had to pick her up on the way home. There was a shortcut from Brooklyn through Forest Park, and I got stopped at a red light just getting out of the park. Now, this was a good area of Queens. As I was sitting there, I saw a car about 100 yards away parked on the wrong side of the street at an angle. Two guys were running towards me, yelling. BOOM, BOOM, two muzzle flashes. Okay, I was not waiting around to see how it all turned out. That was the first shootout I witnessed.

I left Pepsi after about 18 months. It was a good experience, and I made a lot of money. I did a brief stint at a finance company in the Bronx, before I got my job at Chemical Bank in May of 1973.

Chapter 4
Wire Transfer 1973 – 1976

My ex-wife's cousin called me and said that they had an opening in wire transfer, and that I should apply. So, I did, and I got the job. Initially, I was to work in one area. But on my first day, I was told that the Billing Section had just received a "D" audit and that they wanted me to straighten it out. Like I knew anything about billing, audits, wire transfers, or anything else.

It was a pretty straight forward section. We had to send notices to our clients with the charges debited to their account for cables that we sent on their behalf. Back then there were three basic types of communication. A Western Union type cable that was charged per word, much like a telegram or a Telex that we would send, and that was charged by the minute, similar to a phone call back in the old days, and also the bank owned SWIFT System. We would calculate the charge or get the prices per cable from Western Union or another vendor, add fifty cents, and type a debit, credit, and advice ticket. We then had to make sure that all the debits and credits proved out, batch them up, and mail out the advice's. I guess we had maybe 600 to 700 per day, on average.

We would start at 8 a.m. and usually have everything done by 2 p.m., when I would go to lunch. So, more often than not, by the time I got back, I could coast for an hour or even buzz out a few minutes early. We had a seven-hour day until our merger with BankOne. I could usually be home by 5:15 or 5:30. Not a bad day.

The person teaching me the job would also go to lunch at that time, along with one of the typists that worked at another desk, a very sweet Puerto Rican girl, named Lillian. One day we were joined by another Italian guy who was just nuts! As soon as he showed up, Lillian and my trainer took off and left me there with this guy who happened to be a screaming racist. And he was not shy about letting everyone know. So, it being 1973, not much was said, and/or maybe everyone knew him.

One day we were walking down the corridor and he pushed open the door to the ladies' room, turned off the light, and yelled, "Maintenance Man." Now, it just so happened that we had a black racist too. One day

I spied him and the Italian guy having lunch, and they seemed to be having a really good conversation. It turned out that they saw eye-to-eye on a lot of things, as they both believed in the separation of races.

Occasionally I would run into the Italian guy on the Lexington Ave Express. This train ran from the Bronx to the Battery. I would pick it up at 42nd St. Well one time, we were on a crowded train and he was going off about the N——ers and S—-cs. The more I tried to calm him down the louder he got. And I was thinking that no one was going to bother him because he was nuts. They would come for me. Besides that, he was a misogynist too. Back then, most of the HR people were male. In fact, almost all the management were male. Lo and behold, we got a new female HR person. When she came into the room, he began saying, "Hey blondie, baby, baby." And he started following her around.

One time on that same train, there was a homeless guy sitting by the door that led from one car to another. As people would walk through, he would say, "There goes a scumbag." And if they turned to look, "Yeah you. You're a scumbag."

After about six months, the billing section got audited again. And we got an "A." My boss called me over and said that Mr. Martin wanted to see me. So off we went to his office. Mr. John Martin was a big deal in 1973. He was about my parents' age and was the AVP over two departments, Wire Transfer and Domestic Money Transfer, about 100 people. One of the nicest bosses around. Anyway, he thanked me for getting an excellent audit.

And me, Mr. Big Shot at 22 said, "That's good, but what's in it for me?"

Mr. Martin laughed and said, "I don't know. I'll get back to you."

As we left his office, my boss hit me upside my head. "What's wrong with you?"

About a week or two later, my boss came over with an envelope. "You little shit, you got a ten percent raise." That's the kind of man Mr. Martin was, and still is, 96 years young at the time of this writing. I learned from good and bad managers, but I learned to treat my employees fair and genuine from Mr. Martin.

Fast forward maybe 15 years, and John and his wife, Audrey, would host the Money Transfer Golf Outing lunch at their home for many years. I later worked with his son, Doug, in Florida. A beautiful family.

It must have been maybe 18 months or so as a grade seven senior clerk (about as low on the totem pole as it gets), when I got promoted to a grade 10 and moved to the routing desk. I was working with my friend Lillian, mentioned above. Our job was to break down the telex address name, meaning we would type the full name of the bank that sent the telex. We would then read the cable and determine what department to send it to: Foreign Exchange, Foreign Paying and Receiving, Letter of Credit, etc. There were keywords on every cable that we would look for to determine the routing. Once that was determined, we then had to see if there was a test word. We were also starting to get messages via the banking propriety SWIFT system, which was the most secure of all the cable systems.

A test word was actually a numeric algorithm that banks would put on a transfer to verify the movement of money. It would use the amount, the date, a bank code, and sometimes a random number between banks. If a cable did have a test word, we would have to send it to the test men, locked in their little cage. They would then input the various numbers and codes, and if they matched, they would send them to the appropriate department.

There were two ways that we moved the paper around. One was via a color-coded belt that would have various drop points for the test men, tube station, files, and other locations. This was a long conveyor belt that stretched from one end of the department to the other end. The other was a pneumatic tube system that went between floors. We were on the fifth floor, and Foreign Payments was on the sixteenth floor. The tube attendant would gather all the cables for them and put them in the designated tube for that floor and station. It was a compressed air system, so based on the weight of the tube, it would arrive at the correct location. Pretty ingenious system. You had to be sure to drop the tube bottom side down. If you didn't, the tube would tend to open and/or clog the system. That meant holding up payments, and a visit from the tube maintenance man, who would proceed to chew you out.

We had some truly unique characters in those days. First, it was probably 80% or more male. And all the bosses were men. Most of the teletype operators were ex-military because they had the required background in communications. Let me tell you, these guys could type. My old boss told me that he worked near the Soviet border, and they had orders to blow everything up if there was an attack… while they were still there!

One time the boss got a call from the president of the bank. He had a program where he wanted to rehabilitate felons. Now apparently, one could not get bonded to work at a bank if you committed robbery, but murder was okay. My boss was told he was getting a new employee. He was a nice enough guy, always pretty polite and helpful. One day we heard a commotion. Remember the black racist I mentioned above? He got into an altercation with this guy, and we heard, "I killed before, mother fucker, and I'll kill again." As he goes to vault the conveyor belt. Eventually things calmed down, but we were always on the watch after that. We had another guy nicknamed "Jesse the Pipe," as he would carry a pipe as protection on the subway.

My boss interviewed someone for a teletype operator position. He showed up well dressed in a three-piece suit and was qualified. About two weeks later he showed up for his first day wearing a blouse with a push-up bra and skirt. The supervisor went in to see the boss and said that we had a problem and explained the situation. The boss, very ahead of the time, said, "As long as he types fast, who cares." He would switch his wardrobe between male and female.

We had a great mix of black, Puerto Rican, and whites, that all got along great. There were two bars in 55 Water St., and very often on Friday nights many of us would get together. We could really have a great time joking around with each other back then.

The head of Wire Transfer was Mr. G. We did not call him by his first name. He was probably just over 60 at the time, and very old school. Mr. G. fought in WWII, and I think he was a sergeant in Italy. He used to tell us that he could take over NYC with twelve men. How? "Take over the tunnels and bridges." Mister G. would call me "Buffalo Bill" due to my long hair and mustache. I wasn't dressing for success yet.

Once, he went over to a group of guys with a red paper clip and asked everyone where it was made.

My boss answered, "China."

He said, "How do you know?"

Honestly, I don't remember the answer he gave, but it was correct. Mr. G. would always test people like that.

One day, out of the blue, he came up to me and asked, "What high school did you attend?"

"Mater Christi in Astoria."

"What religious order taught you?"

"Irish Christian Brothers."

"Christian or Irish Christian?"

"Irish Christian. You know, with the bibs."

"Me too."

And he walked away. Little did I know that this was the interview for my next job working directly for him. I got the job because I was taught by the Irish Christian Brothers, and because I was Italian. Mr. G. thought I would be shrewd with the money. Interestingly enough, Mr. G. was Irish. So go figure.

I came across the first of many people that embezzled funds from the bank while in that department. These two guys ran the proof in Domestic Money Transfer. If there were small amounts of unclaimed funds, they were taking the money, thinking no one would claim them.

One time, there was some kind of storm or hurricane blowing. Due to the reverse pressure, a couple of windows blew out, taking some cables and wires out the window. We had to figure out what was missing and try to get them resent. This wasn't nearly as bad as the Bond Department that had bearer bonds whisked out the window. They were finding bearer bonds blocks away.

Chapter 5

Due From Banks 1976 - 1978

This job was one of my favorite jobs. One of the perks was that my boss was the head of the department Mr. G. and I was hand picked. I was a grade 13 clerk by then and the very first thing Mr G. told me was that the job was a grade 18, but that HR wouldn't let him promote me to that level. "You have to be a grade 16 first. But you know what, they are going to have to promote you to a grade 18 in six months and give you another raise." Mr. G., the assistant treasurer, was not having anyone lower than a grade 18 report to him. Another great perk was that I got to work on the platform, which was the glass enclosed area where all the officers and officer assistants sat.

My hours were still 8 a.m. to 4 p.m., and Mr. G. told me, "You'll be done by 3:30. If you want, you can leave then, just don't make it obvious. And by the way, you don't go help anyone outside the platform."

"Okay."

The task was simple enough. We had accounts with 93 banks across the country. These banks were used to clear checks, settle letters of credit, pay cash letters, and things like that. Over the course of the month, we had to maintain the "imprest" balance set by each bank. For example, if the imprest balance was $1,000,000 I had to maintain that average for the entire month. What made it tricky was that every two weeks, the "Money Desk" had to balance with the Federal Reserve Bank. Every bank had to ensure that they had an average of 10% of their liquid assets at the Fed. So, the Money Desk traders would need to buy or sell funds on settlement days. If the Fed Rate was high, they would want to sell funds. If it was low, they would want to buy funds. It was a very important job.

Every morning, I would get telexes from the banks giving me the balances and letting me know what was available that day, 1 day, and 2 day. Remember, there weren't any computers that we could just log on and look. I would then make a determination on how much to draw down. But I first had to figure where we were, relative to the imprest, by using a calculator. I then had to either make the drawdown by 3 p.m., for banks outside the NY Fed district, or 4 p.m. in NY. And again, I would have to consult with the Money Desk traders.

It didn't take too long to learn, and the person doing the job before me was still in the department, so I could always ask. On a typical day I was out the door by 3:45 and home at 4:30! Quite a great gig. It was at that job that I met one of my best friends for the last 50 years, Lillian C. Lillian was a hot babe back then, and guys from other departments were always coming around. I used to make up all kinds of stories to send them on their way when she wasn't there.

As I said, this was one of my best jobs, mainly because it was challenging, and I worked independently from everyone else. Not to mention, Mr. G. calling me in to chat when he wasn't busy. One day, I was in his office and the phone rang. Back then, only officers' phones were listed in the corporate directory. Mr. G. answered the phone and asked the guy his name and proceeded to look in the phone directory. His name was not there, and Mr. G asked him, "Who are you?"

"I'm the Clearance Teller at Branch XX."

Mr. G. told him, "I'm an AT. Don't ever call me again."

Another time, one of my old bosses from Wire Transfer saw me there and told Mr. G. he needed to see me. Mr. G told him to come back later.

"Mr. G., it's important."

"Come back later."

My back up for the job was the person who trained me. One day, I had a day off, and when I came back and started collecting the wires, I saw a disaster. Some banks were overdrawn by millions, others that had a low imprest, had a huge sum of money. I was getting irate calls from some banks. So, I asked Jim, "What happened yesterday?"

"What do you mean?"

"The books are a mess. Didn't you cover for me?"

"No, I was out sick."

A little bit later, Mr. G. came over.

"Jim was out. I had to cover for you. I still got it!"

"Yes, sir."

I didn't dare tell him he created a disaster for me. Some banks took months to straighten out. The Money Desk guys were cracking up.

I think I was audited every six months or so. Because of the money involved, it was more often than in most areas. I'll never forget Riggs National Bank. They had a set imprest, and I was told just to leave the balance, no matter what. If I saw any money go in or out, it was a mistake, and I was to fix it that day. One day this auditor, thinking he's some sort of hot shot, was asking all sorts of questions. I told him what I was told, and he said he was going to get to the bottom of the story. I told him, "From what I know, this is a directive from the CEO. I wouldn't ask questions if I were you."

"We'll see about that."

The next day a new auditor shows up. "Where's the other guy?"

"He's gone."

I tried to warn him.

I got to meet a lot of great people around the country doing that job. One great perk was making friends with someone at a bank in New Orleans. She invited me down to stay with her during Mardi Gras in 1976, 1977, and 1978. We had a great time every year.

The first year they asked us what bagels were. Can you believe it? They heard of them, but never saw or ate one. We were trying to explain how they looked like donuts but tasted more like bread. So, the following year, I brought three dozen.

One year they asked if we wanted to attend the "Zulu" parade. "What's that?" They explained that in the early days, African Americans could not march in any parades, so they started their own. It was pretty neat, and besides throwing beads, they also decorated coconuts. I stood there yelling,

"Hey bro, throw me a coconut."

Our friend told us, "This isn't NY. You can't say that here."

We were blown away. It was 1977! We did get some cool beads though.

After one of the trips, I brought back a voodoo doll and pinned it outside the boss's office. We would joke about who it was, but we all kind of knew. One day, my friend Lillian came out of the office and kept jabbing it with pins, as he watched. I think that day he figured it out.

I also met someone from Detroit and I went there a couple of times too. I got to go to the old Tiger Stadium and saw some other great sights.

The original voodoo doll

When I was in this job, I also came across my second embezzler. He was an AVP and he kept the ledger sheets for all the banks that I was making the drawdowns from. He would be on my ass if I was off by a penny and was a real stickler. As it turned out, he took something like a million dollars. The way I heard the story was that he felt he was not being compensated enough, so he decided to make his own salary.

I guess I was in that job for close to two years, when they asked if I wanted to move into a supervisory position in the Outgoing FedWire Section. You Bet! It happened that the person who trained me in the "Due From Banks" area, left.

The person who took over for me was a great guy. He was actually a holocaust survivor and had some unreal stories. He told me about his firsthand remembrance of Kristallnacht. He was lucky in that his mother, father, and sister all survived. He also told me about how the German mothers started to block the trains towards the end of the war.

He got many of us to start investing in the stock market also. He told us that no matter how little you put in, it is going to pay off. "You're young, you have time," he would tell us.

One day I came back from lunch with a Dr. Brown's Cream Soda. For non NY'ers, Dr. Brown's is served in all the Jewish delis. He said that it reminded him of a date he had once.

He proceeded to tell me about the date. He said that he lived in lower Manhattan and that this girl was from the Bronx. When he got there, the girl's mother was telling her to eat. "You need to eat." And she said she was not hungry.

As soon as they got out the door, he asked her,

"Where would you like to go?"

"Ratner's."

Ratner's was a Kosher place in downtown Manhattan, where he lived. So off they went on the subway, and he told me how he had to then take her back to the Bronx later. So, remember Dr. Brown's? He went on to say that he got up to go to the bathroom and there was Dr. Brown's on the table.

"I came out of the bathroom and saw Dr. Brown's."

"Then I see her."

"Then Dr. Brown's."

"Then the backdoor."

"You didn't sneak out the back door?"

"I did. She should have eaten at home."

Another great story was during the high holy days in the Synagogue. You had to purchase tickets to enter, I guess because there were not enough seats to go around. So he told me that they would always hire a big Irish cop to stand at the door. Something happened at home and he had to tell his father. But he did not have a ticket. He explained the situation to the cop, and the cop told him he couldn't go in without a ticket.

"But I just need to go in for a minute. I'll come right out."

"You need a ticket."

"I promise I will come right out."

"Okay, but don't let me catch you praying."

In the 1950s, he enlisted in the US Army. He said that one night they rounded up all the non-citizens and loaded them into trucks. They had no idea, but he was concerned as he had seen this happen in Germany.

Not a word was said, until they pulled up to a courthouse and swore them all in as citizens.

It was just prior to my leaving that job that I was introduced to an AVP that had been around the bank for a very long time. He wanted to automate my job. Nowadays, it would be a piece of cake on a PC, and I could build it in a week. But back then it would have been quite a project. Nick was a great guy and was a parachutist in WWII. He was a bit old school though, and for a young guy like me who wanted things done quickly, he was very meticulous. In any event, several years later we worked on some projects and I have some great stories coming up later.

July 14th, 1977 sticks out as it was the day of one of New York City's blackouts. I was at a friend's, helping to babysit his kids. When I woke up to leave for work, I realized that there wasn't any power. So, I jumped into my car about 6 a.m. and drove about 30 minutes to the office. Since the entire city was down, the Fed declared a bank holiday. The only other person that came in was my boss's boss, and so we spent the better part of the day fielding phone calls from banks across the country. I would guess something like 98 % of the bank staff was not able to get to work.

A few days later, the senior management made an announcement stating that the day would not be a charged absence. I went and asked the boss if I would get a paid vacation day, as everyone else got a day off.

"But you came into work, so you're not entitled."

"But I was here working, while others stayed home. "That should be good for something." It was, and eventually I got the extra day.

Chapter 6

Outgoing FedWire 1978 - 1981

I became a supervisor. Thanks to Mr. G., I already had the title. There was another person that already was working there, and we were to split the duties. A bit awkward if you ask me, but that was the deal. As I was an early bird, I was always there before 8 a.m. My partner did not mind, as he wanted to come in at 10 a.m. The first issue was that he never made it in at 10. He was always late. The boss wanted me to mark late comers down on the timesheet, which made sense, as it was one of the criteria we used in the review. I had no problem with this, but people started to complain to me that my partner was always late, and not being marked. I felt that was a fair point, but it was not my job to manage him. So, I stopped marking people late. I always worked on the premise that I would act and ask questions later. After a bit, the boss asked why I stopped. I explained the situation, and he kept insisting that I start to mark them late. I told him, "You need to mark him late." Eventually and thankfully, he left and the job was all mine.

Our job was to send Fedwire payments out for our clients. These could vary from a few dollars to hundreds of millions. Now they go into the billions. Back then, we could only handle 99 million. So, if a transfer was over that, we had to break it into several payments. We would input the payments into a CRT. We had two machines that created paper tape to hang on the Fed wire MT37 machines that would transmit the payments  to the Federal Reserve Bank. At the same time, another machine would print paper debit and credit tickets, and a paper advice to be mailed to the customer. A clerk would have to check off the numbers printed from these tickets, ensure that all the transfers went out, and that all the tickets were there. It was really a very manual process.

There were two paper tape punches, one for the 3 p.m. deadline and one for the 4 p.m. deadline. The tapes were two different colors, so that when it was close to the deadline you could prioritize them and hang the 3 p.m. first. There was also an art on winding the tape around our fingers, so that they fed into the machine without snagging. The MT37s were loud, and I think we had five of them. The roar was quite deafening when they were all going. And the paper tape punches would buzz every time a new payment was released by a signer from the CRT.

My ears got so tuned that I could hear the paper tape punch jam from across the department. I would go running across the room to stop it, because the more that got caught up in the jam, the harder it was to find the damaged tapes and recreate them. Also, you would have to then reroute from one machine to another if the deadline was approaching. When I first got there, I was allowed to call IBM to fix the punch on my own. Then the data center decided that they needed to have one of their guys come and look at it, so we could waste 30 to 60 minutes. One day the tape jammed and I called the data center (we actually had a red phone that you didn't have to dial). After like 15 minutes, this guy showed up and started roaming around the machine, scratching his head.

"Have you ever seen one of these before?"

"No."

"Then what are you doing here?"

"My boss sent me."

"Get out and tell your boss to send IBM."

Red phone rings.

"Why did you send my guy back?"

"Because he didn't have a fucking clue. Send IBM!"

"Well, he has to learn."

"Then next time you come and teach him." After that they would take my word and call IBM immediately.

We would get payments from various sources. Some would come down the conveyor belt, some would come from other departments via the pneumatic tube, some would be walked over, and believe it or not, some would come by mail. Some would also be called in by the money desk guys on settlement day, every other Wednesday. That would get crazy, and I would just be yelling out transfers to the girls to type. "Hundred million to Chase, Hundred million to Citi," etc. I'd worry about the paper later.

One very busy day I got a call from one department, and he said he had a few transfers left to send out. I told him it was okay, but we were right at the deadline, and I couldn't promise anything. He sent me a tube so packed that I couldn't get them out. So, I sent them back. He called and started ranting and I told him, "Even God couldn't get them out in time." He called my boss and said that he is very religious and was offended.

If we had system problems, we could call the

Fed and ask for extra time. Not something we wanted to do as they would keep records, and abusers would get into trouble. Depending on their mood, they would grant us extensions at 15-minute increments. But we had to have a really good reason and tell them how much we had left to send by dollar amount. Occasionally, they would refuse and if I was really stuck, I'd call Lillian over.

"This is Lillian from Chemical Bank."

"Hi Lillian, what's up?"

"We need fifteen minutes more."

"Okay sure, no problem."

This was after I was begging for 20 minutes!

One day I went to Rockaway beach. It was early on a Sunday and it was pretty empty. As I was walking, I saw this hot blonde babe. So, I figured that looked like a good place to park. It turned out to be Lillian.

"Oh, crap."

Lillian looked over. "What do you mean, 'Oh crap?'"

"I thought I was going to pick up a hot babe, and it's only you!" I might add that Lillian took no shit from anyone. More about that later.

We had a few department heads while I was there. We had Mr. P., that I mentioned during the voodoo doll episode. Mr. R., a good guy that really pretty much left us alone as he was not a payments guy. Mr. A. who was from Foreign P & R, and we could not get away with anything. He knew his stuff and I got to know him very well later in my career. He would break your balls but would listen to you. And finally, Ms. S.

One very funny story about Mr. P. We had an area where banks or companies could call in transfers. Talk about insecure. Anyway, we eventually got a piece of equipment that could record the calls on tape, and it was put into Mr. P's office. It was the size of a phone booth. Mr. P. invited the big brass down to see it. One of the features was that someone could push a button and listen in to a phone call. So, with all the brass in his office, he punched in a button, and they all heard was the clerk cursing out his girlfriend.

The CRTs that we used, 3270s, were big metal boxes that weighed a ton. They also had to be turned off at night or the characters would actually burn through. We all took turns as the late-night supervisor, and one of the tasks was to ensure the CRTs were turned off. Mr. A. always came in early and so did I. So, one day he saw the screens were not turned off.

"Why are the screens on?"

"I don't know. I wasn't the late-night supervisor."

"I didn't ask you that."

I happened to have a piece of balled up paper in my hand, and I thought he had gone into his office. I flung it across the room.

"GET IN MY OFFICE!"

Oops. I thought I was done for that day. But it all worked out in the end, and I was exonerated, getting a reprieve from execution.

Mr. A. was in charge when we had an extremely serious system issue. By that time, we no longer had to hang tape on the MT37s. We had an electronic system in place that would send from our computers to the Fed computers. However, in order to achieve this, we had to implement third party software. Our system and their system had a control number, and they had to remain in sync or the systems would not talk to each other. There was a way for me to resync, but one time I couldn't get it to work.

I called the data center, and they sent over Mike D. He figured it out pretty quickly. He took out a hex calculator and went into some system code and got it working. About six months later it happened again, but Mike was no longer one of our tech guys. They sent over someone else, and I explained to him what happened with Mike.

"I don't think that's the problem."

"Yes, it is."

Now Mike still worked for the bank, and I was imploring them to call him. No such luck. They sent another guy. Then his boss, and then the big boss showed up. Same story every time, and this went on for hours.

Mr. A. called me in with the big boss from the IT department. And I went through the story for the fourth time.

Mr. A. asked, "How sure are you?"

No one knew the system like me. "One hundred percent. It's the exact same issue."

He looked at the IT manager and said, "I think you need to call Mike."

Mike showed up and I told him, "Remember what happened six months ago?

"Yeah."

"It happened again."

Mike took out his hex calculator, and five minutes later, everything worked. The tech guys were pissed off. Crazy huh?

Needless to say, when I took over, I did not know that much. I had been sending wires, but that was it. There were about 24 women who worked in the area that consisted of Fed wires and Bank wires. A little more than half were typists, and the rest were signers. They verified the transaction and released it to be sent to the Fed. It was very slow in the morning and would get more and more hectic as the day went on, especially as the deadlines approached.

It was in that job that I developed a lot of my management style. I always believed that if you treated people fairly, that they would respond in kind. I would always tell them that if they needed to do something for an hour or two in the morning, I'd let it slide, or let them take a half day off. That way, I would usually be able to cover the afternoons. Yes, we would have some abusers, but for the most part it worked out well. Also, if and when we needed overtime, most would stay and help.

One person would come in at 10 a.m., put her stuff down, go to the cafeteria for bacon and eggs, come back and eat, and maybe if you were lucky, she would start working by 10:45. The answer was always, "Well I was here by ten." It took a while to straighten her out.

We did have a couple of guys, including my main man, Leon. He was a hard worker, once he arrived, but he had a tough time keeping on schedule. So I asked him if he wanted to change his start time to 10 a.m., and he agreed. He was still late. One time he came in about 11 a.m.

"What happened?"

"Mr. Robert, there were too many senior citizens on the token line."

"Doesn't that start at ten?"

"Yes."

"So how can you get here by ten if you just got online?"

"I can't fool you, can I?"

The best was the day that he came in and told me that he could not get off the roof, because her husband came home. He had to go up the fire escape and wait for him to leave in the morning. I had to excuse that one just on the premise that it was the best excuse I ever heard.

Several years later, my buddy had to let him go as he was working two jobs during the same hours!

I was always very precise when it came to keeping performance and error records. I wanted the staff to understand the standards, and that they were all being rated fairly and accurately. It was a lot of work back then, as I had to do everything manually. Today, you can just push a button. In the end though, no one could really complain, as I would publish the ratings levels. In later years, when I had to do reviews for IT people, it was much more difficult.

My boss approached me once and wanted me to rate someone excellent. It just so happened that this person was horrible. I refused, and I was told that the big boss wanted to give this person a ten percent raise. I couldn't do it, so he did it and wanted me to sign off. I still refused. In the end they gave the guy the raise, but they didn't say anything else to me. Maybe they thought it was best to just let it die.

I forgot to mention earlier that we had one other method of receiving instructions to send out payments, and that was via a window where other departments could drop off instructions. The person who regularly manned the window was a bit of a gossip and often would get into people's business. I had a young man who was a contractor working for me at the time, and the window clerk started telling people that he saw this guy come out of the ladies room. I don't know if this was actually true.

I looked over and I saw the two of them standing on the platform. I thought to myself, that wasn't good. Another officer was there already but did not know the situation. Just as I got there, the contractor took a swing and hit the window clerk right in the head. My colleague and I grabbed him from the front and behind and looked at each other. We thought, okay now what do we do? I told the guy that security would be there in a minute and he would most likely be arrested if he didn't get out. Needless to say, I called his agency and told them the story. I told them I did not want him working for me and that he should be banned from the bank.

The next day, he had the nerve to call me and start complaining about the ban.

"Do you remember what you told me yesterday, that you did what you had to do?"

"Yes."

"Well, I did what I had to do."

He understood. Wouldn't you know that a few months later I saw him walking down the corridor in the bank. I had to track down where he worked and inform his manager and our HR again that this guy should not be working there.

It must have been sometime in 1979 when Mr. A. called us all in, announcing that he was leaving the department, and our new manager was going to be Ms. S. I was DOOMED. She used to work in Wire Transfer after I moved over to the Due From Banks, and we did not see eye to eye. But to her credit, she was great and none of that ever came up. In fact, she promoted me to Assistant Manager. My first official promotion.

She was always very fair and supportive. I had a guy call me one time very late in the day to get some funds returned from Manufacturers Hanover. I explained to him that it was close to 4 p.m. I could send the request, but they never returned funds the same day, especially this late in the day. But I could try. He said he would get back to me. Meanwhile, I asked one of the typists to get the request ready, so that I could release it as soon as he called back. Instead, this guy called Ms. S's boss's boss, and complained that I wouldn't ask for the money back. Ms. S. came out and asked why. I told her I was waiting for him to get back to me and showed her that I had it all ready. She said, okay, to let it go and come with me. She called this guy and lit him up big time, and then smoothed it over with her boss.

She always defended her staff and always gave us credit for a job well done. Then made sure that the big bosses knew about it. Thas was one of the things I learned from her for sure. After about two years and just before I was leaving the department myself, she was getting promoted and re-assigned. She called me into her office and said, "I have to tell you that you are the only one of my direct reports that never lied to me." That was a real compliment. I never believed in lying to the boss. You always get found out in the end.

She even backed me up against one of her favorites. As the volume increased, she split my area into two and gave him Chemlink. That area ran pretty smoothly, but if they had problems, we would always have to pitch in to help them make their deadlines. The end result was that my staff would always get stuck working overtime and he would not reciprocate. They got slammed and I said, "No." Ms. S. called me and asked why.

"They never help us."

"Go ask and come back."

"They said no."

A few minutes later she came back. "Everyone will stay for as long as you need them today, and any other day that you help them."

We would also get caught up in international political issues. One big one was in 1979 when the US blocked transactions to Iran. Also, around the same time, and I don't know why, we had a special thing going with the Bank of Kuwait. They were assigned two account officers. They would have to walk the transfers from 20 Pine St to 55 Water Street in rain, snow, hail, sleet, or any other weather condition. We would have to create and send the transaction, and then hand them the Fed IMA number, so that they could walk back to 20 Pine and call the bank in Kuwait. As far as I know, that was their only job. I never did find out why.

Towards the end of my tenure there I got home from work and my phone was ringing. I answered and asked, "Who is this?"

"Can you guess?"

Now I really didn't want to play the game, so I started naming all the girls I knew.

"Oh, you know a lot of girls."

Finally, she told me and it was one of my clerks.

I asked, "Why are you calling me at home?"

"I have to tell you something."

"Okay."

"I have trouble working when I see you."

So then, I was thinking to myself, this could be a problem as she was not one of the most stable of people. So then she said,

"If I invite you over for dinner, will you come?"

"That's nice, but I don't really mix business with pleasure." Not quite accurate, but I'm really trying to get off of the call.

"Would you like my phone number?"

"I don't think that's appropriate."

I finally got off the call, and first thing Monday morning I contacted our HR representative. I relayed the story and told him that maybe they needed to find her another place to work. As an interesting side note, about six months after all of that, he got fired for having a workplace romance!

At some point, the Federal Funds traders were looking to hire someone. As I had been working with them for years, in two different roles, they asked me if I was interested. Hell yeah! Their boss felt that I did not have enough college, not that you needed it. He made them hire someone that didn't have a clue, and it took forever for him to get up to speed.

Holidays always had a big impact on that section. In that the day before, we always had a large volume uptick, often as much as a fifty percent increase. We weren't staffed to cope with the volume and so I had to try and get people in early or stay late. We could not just hold over payments. If we did, the bank would have to pay compensation. New Year's Eve, and the day after the Fourth of July, were always the worst, while Christmas Eve and Good Friday were the easiest days. Good Friday was the only day that the Fed would close early.

On April 1, 1980, New York City Transit workers went on strike, and because my area was considered crucial to the bank, many of us were offered hotel rooms for the duration. Mine was up on 34th Street and quite a long walk, which I usually did in the mornings. I then took a car service back in the evening. The bank also gave us per diem for breakfast and dinner and brought in sandwiches for lunch. My sister was working in Manhattan at the time, and the day the strike ended, my brother-in-law to be came and picked us up. Traffic was very slow. At one point, as we neared the bridge back to Queens, one of the urban street people came up to the window and asked if we would like a drink from the bottle he produced, for 25 cents. Richie said,

"No thanks, I can't drink from the bottle."

"I have cups." And with that he took out a sleeve of paper cups. Only in New York.

Another embezzlement story that I heard of at that time was about someone in the International Loan Department. Apparently, he had some kind of gambling debts and was making loans to the mob. He got wind that the FBI was on to him, and he took off on a Caribbean vacation, before turning himself in with a nice tan.

A really funny story was when my friend Lillian went to deposit a check at Chase Manhattan Bank. Now, we were all used to writing payments in very big numbers. She had a check for $1,000.00, and filled out the deposit slip for $1,000,000.00. Rather than simply call her to straighten it out, Chase security contacted the FBI and Chemical security. The Chemical guys all knew her and knew that it was an honest mistake. So did everyone else once they asked a few questions.

One other funny story that Lillian told me was when she was a typist in 1969. The Mets won the World Series, and the Chemical Bank wire department faced Broad Street. Lillian got carried away during the ticker tape parade and tossed all the tapes with payments on them out of the window, and then had to scramble to redo them all before the deadline.

Every once in a while, we would get a call from the CEO's office about a mistake that we made. We had to handle them within 24 hours and report back on what we did to correct the problem. One time, we got a call about someone who would be the future mayor of NYC, where we spelled his name incorrectly. It had no bearing on the payment, but we had to recall the payment, make it again, and be sure that his name was spelled correctly. I did learn, however, that this was the way to get things done in my personal life and used it on many occasions.

Chapter 7

Payments Automation 1981 - 1985

In 1981, I moved to a newly created area called Payments Automation. Prior to this, most of the regulatory and system updates were done by the IT staff, with not a lot of input by the business. Also, management realized that in order to remain competitive, we needed to upgrade our systems.

Our task was to write business requirements and do user acceptance testing for our front end and back-end payments systems. We were also charged with training the staff on updates to existing systems, and when new systems came online. It was a small group with only about six of us, and I was able to recruit one of my FedWire supervisors to the team. We covered both Domestic and International Payments, which at that time had two different systems. We were able to build one system to cover all payments.

Our boss was GK, and she was wonderful. She gave us a lot of freedom and protected us from the management team when systems failed and it was not our fault. Gail worked for Mr. A., so that was a bit of a reunion for me. When we started, there were only four of us, two Domestic and two International. My very good friend to this day, PJ., was already there when I came on board. She was new to the bank and reported to me. After a few months I found that her salary was only $1,500 dollars a year less than mine. So I started looking around outside Chemical Bank.

The most interesting interview was with a Japanese bank. I went to the interview, and I was ushered into a room with about eight Japanese and one American, who happened to be the person that I was to replace. Some of them spoke English, but they were hard to understand. Even so, at the end of the day I thought I did very well. As it turned out, I did. However, the agency called me and told me that the American guy thought I was great, and he was trying his best to convince the Japanese. They agreed that I had the experience, but that I was too young for the job.

Eventually, I was offered a job by Barclays for $25,000, which was a $3,500 raise. When I told my boss's boss, he wanted to know why I wanted to leave. I explained that Paula was new to the bank and making almost the same amount. By the next morning I was offered $26,500. I never did want to leave, so that worked out fine. Right after that the big boss saw me and said,

"We're glad you decided to stay."

I started to apologize, and he laughed. "That's how the game is played."

It was really a great job, with a lot of peaks and valleys. It would be really busy and chaotic leading up to an implementation. Then we would get a break for a bit after the implementation and all the bugs were worked out. At the beginning, everything was hand typed on a typewriter, which made changes difficult, and sometimes we would have to rewrite the entire page. We were able to convince the bosses to purchase a Wang word processor. That was like getting a supercomputer to us at that time. It must have cut the time to process in half, plus we could play hangman.

I had worked with the IT staff in my previous job, but that was much different, as now I had daily contact with them. We were still at 55 Water St., and they worked a few blocks away at 2 Broadway. I always pushed the envelope with them for enhancements that they said were too hard, but we could usually come to a good compromise.

All of Payments was moved to the 16th floor. Mr. A. had a brand new platform area built and I got my first office. This was a large area, and back then every officer got an outside office that faced the street. Not long after that they did away with that practice and put all the offices inside near the corridor. Besides Mr. A. and his direct reports, there was my team and the secretaries.

Two of my very good friends ran the payments areas. Andy Sadler, from the UK, ran International, and another ran Domestic. We would have to interview their people for requirements and train them on the new system. We would create two new systems. One was called Styling, which would take in electronic instructions and format them into a payment. The other, MPES (Manual Payments Entry System), took the place of the two old and different systems used by the two areas. It was a very exciting time in banking.

The Styling system was what I would consider the first step in AI for payments. When messages were received from the Federal Reserve or SWIFT system, it would read the message electronically and put that into a format that a clerk could review and verify. Over the years, banking systems have improved this AI so that 99% of all the messages received can be processed without human intervention. One of the things that does stop for review, are messages that are kicked out for OFAC review. These are messages that US and other governing bodies want stopped for global sanctions. These can be by countries, businesses, or individuals.

It was an incredible amount of work at the time to create and test the code that created this AI. Mistakes could cost a lot of money to correct. If the money went to the wrong place, it could take days or even weeks to get it returned. So the testing was imperative. While thousands of transfers a day might be processed with many different outcomes, we had to develop a way to do this with a small number of transfers, so we could test several times during the course of the day.

Once all the testing was completed and we signed off, the implementation would be done on a Saturday. That was typically an all-day affair. And because it was being done in production, if it did not work, it had to be backed out and done another day. In the beginning, our management tended to overrule our objections to going live in favor of the IT guys. They always claimed that in spite of the issues, they could have it fixed before Monday. Eventually, we got to have the last word.

One day, we were having huge delays in getting the system running. Mr. A. asked one of the lead IT guys,

"What's holding us up?"

"Gravity."

I had to walk away, because if I got caught laughing, Mr. A.'s wrath would head my way. Needless to say, he was not amused, and rightfully so. He went ballistic. But he never asked this guy again, and he would torture the big boss.

We had a very big system overhaul in the works and this same person was in charge of the testing for IT. I wasn't thrilled with this, but there was nothing that I could do. We were to get a jump on testing, and the team came in on a Saturday to start. I was told that everything worked perfectly. Well it didn't. I asked for their results and got a half page of issues. We started to test, and after a few hours of just scratching the surface, we had three pages of major issues. We were leaving early that day anyway as one of the team was getting married. I had just started dating my wife and she accompanied me to the wedding. When I saw Paula that Monday, she said, "Oh boy, when we saw Marian in that tight black dress, we knew you were hooked."

But back to the test results. For some reason, me and Mr. A. were always the first in the office. So he saw me and asked,

"How did the testing go on Saturday?"

"It was brutal. We couldn't get through the first few pages of our testing."

He called the big boss, ranting, and he sent this guy over who wanted to make an issue.

"How about we go into Mr. A.'s office?" He asked.

"He already knows." And I walked out of my office and left him standing there.

A couple of days later the big boss from IT came over to me and asked me to be nice to this guy. I responded by telling him he's a consultant and I'm an officer of the bank. I didn't have to put up with, or answer to, his crap.

Several of the IT guys were from Liverpool, and being a Beatle fan, it was great to ask them about Liverpool and the Beatles. I became good friends with most of them, despite me torturing them about the system not running. Now that is not to say that we didn't have our differences.

One time, IT wanted to do a demo, and I didn't think the time was right. But I insisted on attending.

"Okay, but you can't ask any questions. It's only a demo."

"Okay."

Like five minutes into the demo: "I have a question."

"You're not allowed."

This went back and forth until he walked out and stopped the demo.

I would always push the envelope with the tech guys, like ask for things that are all simple now. For example, I would ask for the number on a queue to turn amber or red as the counts started to increase. This eventually got done as we could see right away if a link went down, and payments were backing up in the queue. Also, sometimes we would have to monitor the queues all day and turn some on and off to get the flow right. I never did get an explanation of why that would happen.

One day my buddy and I were monitoring the queues, and Mr. A. came by and asked, "Do you two morons know what you are doing?"

"Yes."

The implementations were always fun though, even with the long waits. Typically, afterwards we would head out for a meal with the team. One time we had to wait for the batch to run for three hours and headed out for a bar in lower Manhattan. We all got hammered. Finally, we got the call that the batch was done and headed back to the office. Needless to say, we had reports, but no one could read them. One of the guys had to go in on Sunday and check everything, so he left the bar. We kept telling him to take a car home, but he insisted on taking the subway. He barely made it in on Sunday, as he wound up falling asleep on the train and passed his stop, back and forth between the Bronx and Brooklyn.

We also had to report to the auditors, both tech and financial. I had no problem with the financial auditors, because they were charged with ensuring that all the accounting was correct. A few times I had the tech auditor grill me.

"What aren't you asking these questions over at 2 Broadway?"

"They don't have the time."

"And I do?"

"I just need to know what happened on Saturday?"

"So why don't you come in on Saturday and see for yourself?"

I have to admit, I ratted him out to his boss, and from then on, he was part of the Saturday team.

One great story was the production printer issue. For a long time, there was a printer that would just go dead. We could not figure it out for anything. It would always happen at the same time, and we were stumped. Even though we were not supposed to have it, we had our own coffee machine. The management looked the other way because of the long hours, and they wanted coffee too. Finally, we figured out that every morning when we turned on the coffee machine, it would overload the circuit. Somehow our coffee was on the same circuit as a production printer.

Another great coffee story was the day we ran out. The tech guys had the same machine and ordered the same coffee. We sent one of our team to go get coffee from them. We were waiting and waiting. When she showed up, instead of getting some bags for us to brew, she showed up with a full pot of freshly brewed coffee. Iced coffee, that is, as it was January.

With the Styling system, I wrote my first user manual, and I still have a copy to this day. I also wrote the manual for the Manual Payments Entry System (MPES), that was also to be used globally. And I went on my first overseas trip to Hong Kong, but not without some coercion. The person in charge wanted to send someone who knew nothing about the system and wanted me to train her. I protested, and finally said okay, it was fine. "But as they have a 12-hour time difference, when they have a problem at 2 a.m., they can call you or her instead of me." That settled that.

Styling Manual

Business class was not like today. With 14 hours, and only three movies, it was pretty awful. But, I was only 34, so sleep was not an issue. Got there and went right to the top of Victoria Peak. Hong Kong was still under British control and a great place to be for two weeks. The people were great. Whenever I wanted to buy something, they were sure to come with me to get their price, not the tourist price. Mr. Lee Ping came in and measured me for my two suits and delivered them in 10 days. Training went well, but they were hesitant and afraid to make mistakes. I did have those 2 a.m. calls and assured them all would be well. They turned out to have the fewest mistakes out of all the centers. It was not due to my training. They just would not make mistakes.

It had been about 8 years or so since I met Nick, the AVP I mentioned earlier. He was in charge of facilities for our division, so anything having to do with moves or equipment was his bailiwick. The two systems that we used were on two different platforms, and as a result, the staff had to have two machines on their desks. My buddy and I were searching for a solution and came across a company that could toggle back and forth. Thereby eliminating one CRT. After we tested it, and accepted it as a solution, Nick was called upon to do the contract negotiations. And he was one tough negotiator.

The vendor came in to meet with me and Nick. He explained that they could not get the equipment on time and there would be a month or two delay. I told him that it was fine, and we could work around it. Nick said that if I was okay, he was okay.

We went into the big project meeting with about 20 people, and the vendor gave the update about the delay. Nick ripped into him about his not being able to deliver, and that this man (me) had work to get done. He just wanted to get a point across. And he did.

Nick was also good friends with the person in charge of the Officer's Dining Room. Every once in a while, he'd call and say that there was a table open for lunch. We could eat whatever we wanted, but we had to save the cookies and the chocolates for Nick to bring back to the big boss.

Passport 1984

Chapter 8
International Money Transfer
1985 - 1989

I was asked to manage the old Foreign Payments area, now called International Money Transfer. I was promoted to AVP and this was a very big advancement for me. Running my own department. My boss was my first boss from when I first started at the bank, and another good friend was running Domestic Money Transfer. At the top, we had Mr. A., so it was one big happy family.

When I took over, one of the first things I noticed was that there seemed to be a lot of overtime every night, with no supervisors working. They did not get OT. When I dug deeper, I was told that there was not a lot of work in the morning, but they get a lot after 4 p.m.

"So why do we have people starting at 8 a.m. if there is no work, especially supervisors?"

"We always did it that way."

Well now that wasn't the question. In any event, I had them change some hours and told them that as long as there were clerks working, a supervisor had to be present. After a few weeks everything was getting done by 5:30, and there was no more overtime. A miracle.

Back then, the clerks had to rely on books and notes for a lot of the customer information required to complete a payment. Shortly after I arrived, we implemented a new online Customer Information System, but the staff refused to use it. So one morning I arrived early, collected all the books from everyone's desk, and put them in my office. I waited for panic to set in.

The two officers in charge of processing came into my office.

"Someone stole all the books."

"What books?" (Time for a little fun.)

"The ones with all the customer information."

"They weren't stolen. I have them."

So they go to grab them. "What are you doing?"

"Getting the books."

"You can't have them. Use the new system."

"We'll fall behind. We won't get the work done."

"You'll figure it out." They did after a few weeks of pain.

One other quick fix was the staff ratings. I found out that all the supervisors were rated excellent, but none of the staff. I found that odd, especially from some of the work ethic that I was observing. Needless to say, the supervisors were not happy, but the staff recognized the change and they were grateful.

Our job was to process incoming and outgoing US dollar payments for international banks and corporations. These were completed through the Clearing House, and every day there was a settlement in the Federal Reserve Bank. This was to take place between 4:30 and 5:00 p.m. The foreign banks would have to send a payment to us if they were in a net debit position, so that we could then communicate that we settled. This usually went pretty smoothly, and an officer had to be available until this was completed.

One day our system failed, and we could not process over 3,000 outgoing and incoming payments. The problem was between our link to the Fed and our system that posted the transactions to our accounting systems. I was there from 8 a.m. to 11 a.m. the following morning. I then went to a local hotel for a few hours of sleep and came back at 11 a.m.

When I got back, I was in my office trying to explain to an irate account officer what was going on, and that we were doing everything that we could to get everything fixed as soon as possible. The SVP for all of International walked in just as I was wrapping up and offered to rip this guy a new asshole. I refused and told her we had to explain things all the time, and that it wasn't necessary. My buddy from the Domestic area wanted to come over and see what was up, and his boss told him, "I wouldn't go in there if I were you." It took almost a year to get it all settled. I'll have more about this story later.

I was also in charge of the system that routed all the payments for both the International and Domestic Payments. I think it was given to me because of my experience in Payments Automation. No one knew those systems like I did. Even though I was an operations manager at that time, I still had a hand in the automation projects, but as a user.

Back when you could have fun, one of my officer's assistants, Rick, came over to me on a Friday and told me how he and another one of the guys were going to put together a gas grill on Saturday.

"You two guys better get someone to supervise."

"No, Clyde knows how to do this stuff."

Monday when I saw him, he told me that they didn't finish and were going to wrap it up the coming weekend. I did warn him.

The following weekend he came in and asked,

"Robert, we put it all together and when we tried to light it, it just went pssst, and wouldn't light."

"Did you two dopes put gas in the tank?"

"Err, no."

"It doesn't come with gas!"

About two weeks later, he came up to me cracking up.

"I went to a barbecue at my buddy's house on the Fourth. He had a brand-new gas grill. He had all his steaks and sausages laid out, ready to grill. He turned it on, and it goes pssst and doesn't light. I told him, "You moron. You have to put gas in the tank!"

Rick was a good guy and could BS anyone. He was an MP in the National Guard and nominated me for an award as some sort of manager of the year, or something like that.

My friend and I had to come up with a training video starring Rick. It turned out to be pretty funny, but I don't think we could use it, as I was like Jackie Gleason in the "Can it core an apple" episode. "Ummana ummana ummana."

As I said earlier, my buddy and I were both AVPs. Shortly after another member joined the team working for Mr. A. as an AT, bits and pieces were carved out for her. No big deal, we had plenty to do.

However, she was promoted to AVP after six months, and again to VP six months after that. Granted, she was an MBA, but my friend and I had tons of experience in comparison. So, we both went to confront Mr. A., who told us that titles didn't matter, and that we were in the "inner circle." We tried to explain that we would prefer to be VPs, and not just in the "inner circle," to no avail. She was a nice enough person, and although we didn't see eye-to-eye on many things, I believe that many years later at Chase, she saved me from being fired by BankOne people.

Mr. A. knew that my friend and I compared notes all the time, and that since we had similar jobs and experience, he made sure that we were paid the same salary and got the same raises. He knew we could be ball-breakers, and by doing so he had one less headache. We found out the IT guys got bonuses. We approached him and he told us that we can't do what they do. But eventually, he did make the case for us, and got us bonuses.

One day, he walked into the Domestic department on a Friday, and saw people in casual dress. When my friend arrived, he was summoned.

"Is everyone on vacation?"

"No, why?"

"They are dressed like it."

"It's dress down Friday. It's good for morale."

"Not, mine." That was the end of that.

My friend and I needed a printer for a PC one time, and they were hard to come by. We knew that the boss had one that was never turned on. So, we went into his office to check it out one day when he was out. His secretary saw us and wanted to know what we were up to. The printer was locked up, so we needed to convince her that he would never figure out that we swapped out his good printer for a broken one. He never did.

Mr. A. could break'em with the best of them. One time he asked one of his direct reports to call the car service. It went something like this:

"They said one hour?"

"An hour."

"Sorrentino called Hello, it's Sorrentino, I need a car to China, five minutes, okay."

Now the truth is one of my team had an 'in' with the car service company. All we had to do was mention her name, and we were at the top of the list.

In those days we could also print official checks as a form of payment. Access to the floor was not nearly as tightly controlled as it is today. People could go up to the 16th floor to pick up the check with proper ID. One of the supervisors came over and said,

"There's a guy at the window to pick up a check."

"What's the problem?"

"He says his name is Saint John."

"What does the check say?"

"Saint John."

"And his passport?"

"Saint John."

"I guess he's Saint John. Give him the check."

I was authorized to sign checks. But when the check was printed to buy our home in 1986, I had my boss sign it, just in case we got to the closing and someone noticed that I was the recipient and signer.

It was also around this time that I went on my first trip to the UK. I loved London, and later in my career I spent a lot of time there. I reunited with my buddy, Andy, and during the trip my wife was able to come over too. There was even a mention of me getting a role in Cardiff, Wales, but that never transpired.

The best Mr. A. story was when we were in the market for a system to track and process investigations. He called in the "Inner Circle" to make the final decision at 2 p.m. It was myself, my friend, my boss, and the other VP in the group. He proceeded to tell us that we had one vote each, and that my buddy had two, because his boss was out. However, he had six votes, and it had to be unanimous. So now you see where this is going.

He went around the room and asked everyone for their vote. Note: He was saving his vote until the end. So it was one for Pegasystems, and four for the other choice. We went around for about an hour. We took another vote, and my boss caved about 3:30 as he had a bus to catch at about 4:45. So we were two for, and three against. About 4 p.m., my boss gave me the high sign, like "I gotta go," so I changed my vote. My buddy was still holding out with his two votes. My boss was holding up signs, "Just say yes." Finally, at about 4:30, my friend caved and Mr. A. casted his six votes for 11 to zero.

"Remember, it was unanimous, I don't want any complaints later."

For about the last year in International, I was moved from my role in Payments and put on Special Projects. One of the projects was to work with Pegasystems to create the new Investigations modules. That was a lot of fun and I got to go to Boston several times.

While I was in that role, there was a problem at the end of the day where 34 payments got rejected by the NY Clearing House. While we still had a chance to affect the payment through the Fed, my boss called me over and told me that no one could figure out what happened, and they were not sure if the payments were made. As I said earlier, no one knew the systems like me. I took a look and saw that, for some reason, our system reset back to one and the payments were numbered one through 34. I explained to everyone that they did not clear, that's why they were rejected, and we should just pay them. Well, no one believed me. So my boss asked me, "Are you sure?"

"Yep, I'll stake my career on it. You can call the banks that were supposed to get the funds."

They called a couple and they confirmed that they did not get the money. Well, the head people in IT weren't convinced, nor was anyone else. So, they kept us around until midnight, trying to convince me that I was wrong. They did this whole white-board thing, with all kinds of numbers, for like an hour. And in five minutes, I showed them that they were wrong. With glazed looks on their faces, they decided to keep programmers to run comparisons against our front end and back end systems. My boss and I headed over to the hotel. As I walked into the office at 8 a.m., my boss was there.

"They found a difference. How many do you think?"

"Thirty-four didn't go out."

"Yep."

Needless to say, there were a lot of "I told you so's" handed out.

By the end of my tenure at Chemical Bank, we were still digging out of the big systems disaster I mentioned above. I guess a little more than a year had gone by and we had about a 12 million credit on the proof, and the Foreign Exchange department was missing 10 million. I had my doubts that our difference was part of theirs, but the management teams decided to give them the money. Not two days after that happened, Bank of Tokyo made a claim on us for 10 million, and we gave it away.

There was a half-assed attempt at balancing it out, but the final document still showed a difference. I was given the job of doing a reconciliation, and not only did I prove that we should not have given FX the money, I balanced everything out. At some point, the head auditor came to me complaining that I was undermining their work. I told him, not only was he wrong, but he signed his name to an inaccurate proof. "So don't come complaining to me."

Once it was all done, Mr. A.'s boss called me in, and had me go over my findings with a numbers guy friend of his. We then had to present it to the SVP in FX, Tony H. He was known to be a brilliant trader and not one to trifle with. He was also my buddy Andy's first big boss in the UK. In any event, I bundled up all my documentation. Mr. A. and my boss headed uptown to his office. There were three of us and three of them, and Tony was not looking happy. I was told it was my show.

For about 20 minutes, every time Tony's people made a case, I presented documentation to counter them. Tony would ask them for their documentation, and they had none. They were so sure they were right; they didn't prepare. Tony was starting to boil and finally got up and said, "I've seen enough, get out."

I looked at my bosses, and they were already headed for the door. His guys got up and started to go and we heard,

"Not you too, sit down."

Needless to say, I was a hero for a few days.

It was in that job that we had another person who embezzled funds. He was in charge of the Compensation Area and would find a case and make up a fraudulent payment. Then he would send it to an account in another bank in his wife's name. He would have a clerk type the payment and ask for it back, saying that he would check and release the payment. This went on for quite some time, until one typist could not read the instructions and asked her boss to check it out. He realized that it was fraud right away and went to his boss. After a weekend, we discovered that at least $380,000 was taken.

In early 1989, I still wanted to be an IT manager. I went to an interview with Chase, and got the job! I had been offered a really great job in Operations, but I was bored and felt that I could manage IT projects better than most. I actually said that I would take the job, with the caveat that I would have one of the better junior officers be my right hand, and they agreed. He was very happy for a couple of days, until I announced I was leaving. He tortured me for years after, but he actually did very well with my replacement. We were reunited in Tampa some 12 or so years later.

Chapter 9

Chase Manhattan Bank ITEX
1989 - 1994

I have to start this story with my interviews. After the initial interview with Human Resources, I had a very pleasant interview with my boss to be, Mr. S. He was a very refined Indian gentleman, and we got along just fine. I then was asked to also interview with two of his peers. They interviewed me together. They were good guys and felt I had a lot of knowledge, but then asked the question,

"Well, you are not trained in systems. What if you come across a problem and you don't know what to do?"

"I'll call one of you." They cracked up and gave me a passing grade.

Finally, I had to meet with Mr. S.'s boss, Mr. D. Now he was one the most unique managers that I ever had. I would not necessarily rate him as one of the best, but he knew how to get things done, and had a sort of sixth sense about things. Also, he was one of the funniest businessmen I ever met. I have several stories to prove it. I guess we spoke for about 30 minutes or so, and finally he said,

"There's no question you know the payments business, but I'm concerned that you never managed a systems project."

I said, "Didn't you just tell me that you fired two tech guys who were managing the project because they weren't getting the job done? You have plenty of tech guys. You need someone like me to manage them, not another technician. If I don't get the job done, you can fire me in six months."

"You're right, you're in!"

About a year later we were in a meeting and he told the story and said that he hired me because I was confident that I could do the job, and that he could fire me if I didn't. The he added,

"When I tried to fire him after six months, HR told me that I would have had to fire him in three!"

My orientation day was pretty funny too. I guess there were about 20 of us in the room filling out the forms and such, and in the middle of all of it, security came in and marched one of the guys out. About three days later, he came in looking for me. I was his new boss! R was from Cuba, and there was some sort of SNAFU with his papers. He was a citizen and a Vietnam War "tunnel rat, so I'm not sure what happened. In any event, he was one crack Assembler Programmer. He would put the so-called expert to shame. For those not familiar, Assembler is a very difficult machine language from the early days of computers. Sometimes I would hear all this foul language coming from his cubicle.

"What's up?"

"I give it shit, it gives shit back, and tells me to get the fuck outta here!" Very technical indeed.

Mr. S then took me around the operations area to introduce me to the managers there, and we came across Mr. R. Sam introduced me and Mr. R.. said,

"Just what we need around here, another fucking systems guy."

Mr. S. started to apologize, and told me that when he started he told him, "Just what we need around here, another fucking Indian."

I explained that I knew of him from Chemical and no big deal, I've heard worse.

In my first briefing, Mr S. told me that the system was basically done, and we just needed to test and to go see the head programmer, and my good friend of over 30 years. Ara and he could give me the details. So, I was a tester. I went to see Ara and he told me there was no code, just "stubs."

"What's a stub?"

Ara explained that there was some basic code that worked independently, but there wasn't a system to speak of. He then went further to explain that half the staff didn't have a clue. So I had to go explain this to Mr. S. I think we were still like a year away.

There was another consultant that we nicknamed, the Tasmanian Devil, as he could code, but the man, was either on or off. However, he was good for me in meetings, because I worked out a signal that I could give him when I didn't understand something, and he would rephrase it for me. After about six months in IT I realized that no one else knew what was going on either. One thing that I did as an IT novice was ask a lot of questions, such as, "Why did you have to go through steps 1, 2, 3, 4, and 5? Couldn't you just skip 2, 3, and 4? Oftentimes you could.

Eventually, I was able to replace the staff with good people of my own and we did finally get it completed. We became one of the star systems.

One day I got a call from HR asking me if I knew one of the senior managers from Chemical Bank. It just so happened that I knew him very well, as he would come to me all the time with questions about payments. They wanted to know how he got along with people, and I said great, but that he might not get along with the senior management. Anyway, to this day I don't know why they called me about someone that was at least three levels above me.

Fast forward about a month and Mr. D. came into my cubicle.

"Bob, how are you today? Can I get you a coffee? Buff your shoes?"

"What?"

"Your friend from Chemical is the new big boss. Call me if you need anything."

After his arrival, the new big boss called in me, Mr. S, and Mr. D. He started ripping into us about system delays. He was ranting and raving for about a half an hour. As we were leaving, he called out,

"Bob, wait one minute, that wasn't meant for you. But I had to have you here. I know you know what you are doing."

Six months later, I came back from vacation and Mr. D. came into my cubicle.

"You're a nobody, I spit on you, your boy is gone."

I told you he was a funny guy.

His secretary was known for keeping tight control of the supplies. She was on her way out for vacation and he threw open the supply cabinet and started shouting,

"SHE'S ON VACATION, GET YOUR PENS, PADS, AND SUPPLIES!"

Another time he handed her a million dollar lottery ticket and asked her to check the numbers. She started yelling, "You won, you won!"

"How can that be? I bought the ticket this morning" He got the numbers from the night before and played them just to be a ball breaker.

He was truly amazing though. Several times I saw him come into a meeting late and pick right up. One time he walked in just as someone was finishing a technical question addressed to him. He may have heard the last sentence, and he gave the perfect answer.

Once we went into production with ITEX, I found myself in the line of fire when the system went down, as opposed to being the user waiting for the system to come back up.

Several disasters come to mind that took quite some time to fix. The first was the time when the system just stopped. It was an exceptionally busy day and we were stumped. Ara couldn't figure it out and was in constant contact with one of the database specialists. Eventually she told us that we hit the "high water mark." Now, Ara had never heard of this and was searching all the manuals for that term. What actually happened was that there was a system counter that we were using to assign sequence numbers. That counter was based on a hexadecimal number and stopped at 32,767 or around that number. Once Ara finally realized what she meant, he was able to get around it to start the system again. Then figured out the long term change so that it would not happen again.

I don't recall the exact issue one other time, but it was going on for hours and we could not figure it out. We had all the bosses hanging around, with the new big boss on the phone. Eventually, we thought we had a fix to try and the data center kept pressuring us for a percentage of certainty that it would work. We had no idea but felt that we had to try something. Finally, the boss told them, "If my guys want it, just do it." We appreciated the support, and it did actually work.

It was always disconcerting to come back from lunch and see five or six of my staff standing around a computer screen.

"What's up?"

"The restart file is corrupted, and we need to replace it."

"So, what are you waiting for?"

"The data center won't let us; they just keep restarting the system."

I got on the phone and asked, "How many times are you going to do the same thing that doesn't work? You need to replace the file."

"You'll lose all the data."

"No we won't."

"Yes you will."

"No we won't. We do it in tests all the time."

"Don't blame us."

"Just do it already." Fifteen minutes later all was well.

For some strange reason, instead of putting in a proof module from the start, the bosses wanted us to build a separate system. It was a dog, and after maybe a year, they told me to incorporate it into ITEX. It really wasn't that hard. The day it was going into production, I casually mentioned to the lead user tester something about the proof report, and asked if she tested it. She said yes, and I asked if she checked it? The online system was working well, but just as I walked in the door at home in NJ, my beeper went off. Uh oh. So, I called the person who we left behind.

"What's up?"

"Is the proof report supposed to be all zeros?"

"No."

"Well it is."

We tried for a while to fix it from home, but eventually we all had to head to Manhattan. It must have been early in the morning when it was done, but I figured we'd better hang around. I left the person in charge of the proof in the operations area. At about 1 or 1:30 I asked him if he needed a sandwich and brought one back for him. The second in command of operations, Mr. R., came over to me and said,

"We don't allow the staff to eat at their desks."

"He's not your staff and it's not his desk."

One of my buddies came over and told me that he wasn't happy with my answer.

"Tell him the next time the system goes down in the middle of the night, he can bring his ass in to fix it."

When that all happened, my old boss, Mr. S. had left and I was reporting to his boss and attending her staff meetings. I was the only AVP, and when she asked what happened, I just told her that we messed up. We knew what we missed and were putting things in place to ensure that it didn't happen again. The rest of her reports looked at me like I was nuts for admitting that we screwed up. Her boss, Ms. L., called me and thanked me for fixing it.

"If we didn't screw up there'd be nothing to fix."

"You got it done, that's all that matters." I always had a great relationship with her.

A couple more Mr. R. stories: One day I had to ask him a question and I went over to his desk and he was reading a newspaper. "Can I ask you a quick question? What is today? The 21st?"

Exasperated, he looked to his secretary and said,

"Tell him what day it is." "It's Thursday. On Thursday mornings he likes to read the Irish Echo. If you come back this afternoon, he'll gladly answer your question."

Another day, he had just come back from Hong Kong, and he told me the following story:

We booked a junket to take the Indian bankers to Lan Tau island for dinner. Now there are no drinks in the restaurant, so I had a few cases of beer put on the boat. Let me say that there are two kinds of Indians: the vegetable eaters, and the fish eaters. The fish eaters don't drink. When we got to the restaurant, I had to take a leak, and walked all the way back outside the building.

When I got back, "Where do you think I have to sit?"

"I don't know."

"Between the head Indian and his wife, fish eaters, and they ain't drinking."

Being an old user tester myself, I was always a stickler for testing. That being said, we had one guy who was a major pain in the ass. One of my staff was always getting into arguments with him and finally I told him, "Do me a favor, don't argue. If he gives you any shit call me from the phone booth on the street."

My phone rang.

"Bob, it's G."

"Where are you? It sounds like you're in the street?"

"I am, you told me not to argue."

What happened was that this person came over to him and told him that the printer was out of paper, and G. told him to put paper in it himself. Anyway, an argument ensued, and he called my boss. I explained to my boss that this person was a real pain and was always looking for a fight. I went on to explain further that we all changed the paper when it ran out, and it took only a minute.

Mr. S. told me to call him, and the three of us would meet. Being the nice guy that he was, Mr S. explained and told him that it was no one's job to change the paper, and that even Bob changed it when necessary. He went on to say, "You know I don't know how to change it; Let's go out there together and Bob can show the both of us."

He told my boss, "I don't have to sit here and take this bullshit."

Mr. S. exploded. "Get out, get out, and never come back again!" That was the only time I saw him explode.

"What's his problem?"

"I told you so."

I think it was late 1991 or early 1992, that our department was one of the first to move from Chase Plaza in NY to Metrotech in downtown Brooklyn. That was a real bummer, mainly because it added about 15 minutes to my trip from NJ. In NY, I could just get off the bus and walk about half a mile. The first Friday that we were there, I was on my way out and stopped to hit the bathroom. As I left, the door handle came off in my hand. Now I was thinking that I was going to be stuck there until Monday. Thankfully, after about 10 minutes someone else came in and I was yelling, "Don't let the door close!"

Eventually, we had one of the best systems in the group and we consolidated the International and Domestic systems. I was still an AVP and all my peers were VP's, and I was really pushing for a promotion. The boss walked over one day and casually mentioned that there was a VP position in England, and that Ms. L. wanted me to go. But they knew that we were trying to adopt, and probably wouldn't want to take it. I told her that we had no idea when, if at all, we would get a case.

So she said, "You'll go?"

"If my wife agrees, yes."

My wife was working for Dean Witter at the time, and after we discussed it, we decided that we would go, if I got the job. I was sent over for a couple of in-person interviews. I was supposed to meet with my direct manager first, but he got tied up and I wound up meeting with his boss first. That was a bit disconcerting, but there was nothing I could do about it. Anyway, he asked me a bunch of business questions and finally he asked, "So, what makes you think that you can pack up, leave your family and friends for two years, and do a good job?"

"Well, I think very highly of myself and my capabilities to the extent that some may consider me an egomaniac." Why I answered like that I still don't know, I did not know him at all.

With that he popped up, slammed his desk, and said, "I know exactly what you mean, you're going to do great."

He had the same personality! I then did meet with my boss, Tim, and he was one of the best bosses that I ever had. Little did I know that these interviews were pretty much a formality. I was then told that I could make another trip with my wife to have a look around before making a decision. We did find a place and the wheels were set in motion. When we arrived at the hotel, there was a big bouquet of flowers for my wife, and she said, "It's going to take a lot more than that."

After we got back, I had to bring her into my HR department as they wanted to be 100% certain that we both agreed to go. After signing a bunch of papers, they explained all the perks and monetary payments, most of which I had an idea about. At the very bottom, however, there was a large number. "What's that?"

"That's your moving bonus, tax free, three months salary."

"When do I get that?"

"You can have one month tomorrow, and you get the next two when you get to the UK. Would you like me to credit you the money?"

"Yes."

They agreed that my wife could stay and work in the US for six months and they would cover my housing in the UK. My wife was so well liked at Dean Witter that they agreed to hold her job for a year.

Just prior to all of this, Ms. L. wanted each Tech area to film a little skit to explain what they do. I put one of my guys in charge, and like me, he was a big Marx Brothers fan. So he came up with the idea to recreate the stateroom scene from "A Night At The Opera." It was a real stretch, but it went over great, and we had them rolling in the aisles. I was Groucho.

Chapter 10

Chase Manhattan Bank Bournemouth 1994 - 1996

In September, I was off to England, and it was exciting and distressing at the same time. It wasn't easy to leave my wife alone in the house in NJ, and I was constantly worried, especially if I couldn't get her on the phone.

Our first home was a lovely place on a lake in Ringwood. The view from the back was spectacular, and you could usually see a few swans swimming. It was just a short ride into town, and it was much different than the US. First, there was a brewery, which was pretty cool, but also it was a throwback in time, as there was the butcher, the baker, and the fishmonger, all in little shops. There was even a Woolworths.

Passport 1994

It was about a half hour or so drive into the office in Bournemouth, which was a little campus. The original home, Littledown House, was still there, which was used for meetings. Then we had a pretty big building with offices, and another building that housed the gym and cafeteria. Back then, most of the banks at least had a bar or a pub in the building or on campus. I liken back to an old Abbott and Costello movie where they pushed a button and the room turned into a casino. Cafeteria by day, pub by night.

My boss, Tim, was just wonderful; anything I needed, he was there for me. Technically, I was not supposed to have a company car, as all the other officers did, because I was an expat. Tim jumped right in and argued that I could not sell my car in the states, because my wife needed it. They gave me the car. A big part of the deal was the promotion to Vice President. When the promotions came out, I was not on the list. I was really upset, and Tim said, "You are, it doesn't matter." But it did and he knew it. Somehow, he got it done, and in a week or so I did get my official promotion.

I really had a great team, and I am still very good friends with many of them almost thirty years later. One of the first things that I did when I got there was to have a breakfast meeting, which we would do all the time in the US. To them it was a bit strange, but they thought it was a nice gesture. In the cafeteria, we could get a nice full breakfast, but I usually would get a bacon or sausage buddy (sandwich), which was, I think, only about a pound, or one pound fifty. Lunch was another story, there was really no place around that we could walk to, so we were at the mercy of the cafeteria. My favorite days were when they were serving bangers and mash, or shepherd's pie. Sandwiches were okay, but very lean on the meat and cheese, and hold the butter. There was a sports center down the road, that we could walk to through the back gate of our property, and they served beer and wine. I would get some food, the Brits two pints.

I was allowed one paid trip home in business class a year, but Tim always found a way to get me back home more often on some kind of business trip. I was able to fly back home for my parents' fiftieth wedding anniversary in October of 1994, and then came back for Christmas that year too. The longest stretch away was from January of 1995 to March of 1995, when I went home to pick up my wife to bring her back to England to live.

One really nice thing in England was that people still dressed in tuxedos for events like the Christmas Party, New Year's Eve, and the like. The night before going to the airport to pick up my wife, there was a boxing event at the sports center, black tie of course. I bought a tux, because I got a special invitation as one of the few Americans. Well, we started off at the pub, and then I had been told that it was the tradition to order some wine for the table. I ordered at least one, maybe two, but so did everyone else. Needless to say, it was a long ride to the airport ninety miles away the next morning.

Speaking of the pub on campus, most would stop for a beer or two on the way out on a Friday night. I would, especially as there was not that much to do when I got home anyway. The first couple of times, I would have two pints and I was floating. Finally, I realized that the English pint was twenty ounces and their ales were much more potent. I stepped down to a pint or a pint and a half. My friend, Jon, was ordering shandies, and I said, "What's that?" It was beer and lemonade (7UP). I was not a fan.

On the flight home, I felt something going on inside my mouth. Luckily, I was able to get to the dentist quickly in the states to find that I had an abscess and needed a root canal. Oh, boy, he told me that he could start it, but I would need a dentist there to finish. I called my secretary in the UK and told her that I was not a fan of any dentist, but I needed one in Bournemouth. They found me a really good one and it was like a tenth of the cost.

When we got to our home in Ringwood, there was for sale sign up; we were supposed to have it for a year. We did get some extra time, but it was crappy to get back and have to start house hunting again.

We did eventually find a place in Ferndown, which was a little closer to work. Not the best home, but we could walk to the small-town center, and it was pretty close to the Tescos just down the road. It was smaller and we had to deal with a lot of issues, including a flea infestation, but we had wonderful neighbors on either side, who sort of adopted us. On the right, were Gerald and Trish, who I would classify as the party people. There was always something going on there. On the left, were Harry and Beryl. Harry was a retired army colonel and Beryl had also served; I believe as a captain. Marian and Beryl hit

Harry and Beryl with Ashlee

it off just great, and it was comforting for me to know that there were good people next door when I was traveling.

Prior to all the EU stuff, the Brits could ferry to France and pick-up duty-free booze. Gerald would make that trip often and asked me if I needed anything. He was a master at loading the car with consumables. At that time, we had our Shih Tzu, Ashlee, and Beryl came by and wanted to know if she and Harry could take her on their walks. Later on, they insisted that they take care of her when we went on vacation. She became the queen of their household, and they even named their home "Ashlee Cottage."

One day I ran into Beryl in the garden, and she asked,

"Have you seen the man looking for his little dog?"

"No, I haven't."

"I don't believe that he lost his dog. You know when people from Liverpool are in the South in the summertime, they are up to no good."

I had a good laugh telling that to my Liverpool friends. We did join the neighborhood watch, not because of the incident, but we just thought it would be a good idea, especially with all my travel. We only got one call, to beware of hooligans in the area. Beryl and Harry were so special and we were so sad to leave them. Beryl gave my wife a parting gift of one of her prized teapots.

In the summer of 1996, when our son was only a year old, Gerald came by and told me that we must go with them to a picnic event, and that Trish, he, and all of their friends hired a bus to drive the hour or so. We were very hesitant because of the baby, but he finally convinced us, and the daughter of my buddy, Les, from Chase said she would watch the baby. In fact, she and her mum came over. We were blessed with so many wonderful people in the UK.

Every year this event had a theme, and everyone was to go in costume. They also had kiosks set up with the theme, and the entertainment was from West End shows with professional singers and dancers. The year we attended was "Oriental", so we had to dress the part. I had a friend from Vietnam who was headed there, and she brought my wife back beautiful silk pajamas for only two pounds.

Now that is not all, some people had champagne, tablecloths, and other kinds of finery.

Some families came dressed alike or had a theme. Did I mention there were 5,000 in attendance? In the best of British tradition, the ale was flowing. Again, two of the loveliest people, and great friends.

To this day, I am still very close with my friend, Jon, and his wife, Quita. They visited us in Florida, and I visited with them a couple of times while on business trips to the UK. Jon did the same when we were in NJ. As I mentioned, my wife came in March of 1995, and I think we moved to Ferndown in June. I think our first guests were Jon and Quita. We were just shooting the shit, and Jon said something about work and Quita said to me, "That's a real compliment considering Jon doesn't fancy Americans."

I made sure that when Jon came to NJ, that I showed him the British Retreat Route.

At that time, Jon was not a good airline passenger, and I used to spook him all the time on the plane. "What's that sound!" We were coming back from Paris, and we were in a small jet flying through a really bad storm over the channel. The pilot was making the announcements in French first and then in English. Jon kept turning around and finally I asked why.

"I want to see if the French are panicking."

Another time, we were coming back to the UK and there was a very chaotic queue. I told him to follow me, and I ensured that we got up close to board first. That was very un-British of me.

In June of 1995, we received word that our son, Matthew, was born in Jacksonville Florida, and we had to get a quick flight to pick him up. Then we got to NJ and got him a passport and a visa to enter the UK. Once again, Tim was just wonderful. He told me to take as much time as

I needed and not to worry about work. He said that this was a family event and that my number one concern was to get all of this sorted out. When we did get back, he and his wife had a crib and other things for us to pick up and use for as long as we needed.

About six weeks later, we had to return to NJ for some adoption details, and while I was there, Tim asked if I could make a quick trip to Puerto Rico for a couple of days. While I was there, on a treadmill, I saw the Chase and Chemical logos pop up on CNN. I thought to myself, merger? Sure enough, later that day we all got the official word. So, six years after leaving Chemical Bank, I was part of the family again.

The system that I was working on was very similar to the payment and routing systems that I worked on in the past. The big difference was that we had to account for several currencies and clearing systems. In addition, we had to account for currency conversions and regulations from multiple central banks across Europe. We also had a front end created and maintained in-house, and a back end that communicated to the other banks. The back-end system was built by a firm in Frankfurt Germany, and as a result I made several trips there.

An issue with this system resulted in my getting chewed out for the first and only time. I learned of an issue with this system where a programmer could get into the production system and potentially cause harm or appropriate funds. Normally, I would raise this with Tim, the head of Payments IT before notifying anyone else. For some reason, I brought this to the auditor. By the time it got back to Tim, it was blown way out of proportion by the operations manager and the auditor. They were reporting that somehow, we were at fault, as opposed to identifying and reporting a potential issue. Once Tim learned the real story, he went all the way to the top to straighten it all out. It did not help that he and the ops manager did not always see eye to eye.

A few days later, the auditor came over to me and tried to smooth things over by telling me that he did what he did to protect the bank. I told him "No, what you actually did was ensure that if someone sees a problem like this, don't say anything because you are going to blame them."

About a month later I had a chance to see the big boss in America, and as soon as I walked in, she said, "I know, I took care of it." But in the end, I was transferred from Tim to the operations manager in 1996. We got off to a rocky start, but it all worked out in the end.

Two big things started to happen in late 1995 and early 1996. The merger, of course, and they wanted to create an International ACH system in Europe. The original idea was to build this completely from scratch. I protested and said, "We have an ACH system in Tampa. Why do we want to start fresh? Let's at least talk to them and see if we can use or replicate what they have." To my surprise, senior management agreed, so I sent one of my staff to Tampa to investigate and report. More about this later.

Mergers are always a power play, and which systems are going to be selected are always a crap shoot. In some cases, the best ones win out. In other cases, it's very political. Because Chase had a more formidable presence globally for payments, we won out. That being said, in my opinion, Chemical had the better system in the US, but Chase won out there. Trying to merge these systems and deal with DDA conflicts and rules was extremely difficult. As a result, special teams were formed to do the work and systems staff were really put to the test. They had to work long hours and weekends.

One day Tim came over to me and asked, "Do you know Tony H. from Chemical Bank?"

"Do I ever!" And I proceeded to recount the FX story and told Tim.

"You'll know exactly where you stand."

Tim came back from the meeting and told me that I could not have been more right.

I did get a chance to meet Mr. H. in Bournemouth and was introduced as a Chemical guy from NY. He didn't seem to remember our encounter above, and I sure wasn't going to remind him.

In June of 1996, we invited many of our Chase friends to Matt's first birthday party. One of my staff had been commandeered to work on the merger. As soon as Tim saw his wife, he went right over to her and apologized for making her husband work long hours, but that he would be compensated when it was all over. I thought it was one of the nicest gestures I ever saw a senior manager make.

One of the best parts about being in the international area of a company was that we got to travel around a lot. Together, my wife and I went to France, Spain, Italy, and Belgium. I also made a few trips to Hong Kong, as well as Germany, France, and Italy on my own. One of the most fun things I did was an IT cruise on the Oriana, a brand new cruise ship. It was basically a cruise to nowhere for three nights, where you went to presentations, met with other IT folks, and things like that; a conference at sea. Now, let me tell you, the booze was flowing, and after the second night the captain announced that we were making an unscheduled stop to replenish, as they went through more alcohol in two nights than they normally do in two weeks. I don't think some people even slept.

Just before returning home in October of 1996, it was pretty much agreed that we would use the Tampa ACH process for the international hub. A big meeting was held in London at the Dorchester Hotel, hosted by my old boss, Mr.D. I was going up from Bournemouth and I invited my guy, Andy, to come with me. He told me that it was his anniversary and asked if it was okay if he brought his wife up for the two nights. I said, "Sure, it's not going to cost anything extra for the hotel." So that first night there was a cocktail party, and Mr. D. saw Andy and gave him a warm greeting. Then asked,

"Who's this with you?"

"My wife."

"YOUR WIFE!" I didn't know that you were married. You weren't wearing a ring in Tampa and you were looking for the "T and A" bars."

Needless to say, Andy got some earache from his wife. Of course, none of this was true.

The next day, I saw Mr D.

"You got Andy in big trouble, and it was his anniversary."

"You think I need to apologize and buy them dinner."

"I think that would be nice." Which he did and confessed that it was just a funny story.

One of my best mates there was Les. He was a cockney lad, and he and his wife were always so gracious. In fact, when he found out that we were going to be alone for Christmas, they invited us over to be with their family for a traditional Christmas dinner. They even had gifts for each of us, as was their tradition. I got to go on several trips with Les and it was always great fun. He would teach me cockney rhyming slang, and my gift was a dictionary of the slang. It works as follows: There are two words. The first word is what you say, the second word rhymes with what you mean to say. Example:

Trouble and strife = wife
Dog and bone = phone
Iron hoof = poof
Merchant banker = wanker

So if you want to say that your wife is on the phone: "The trouble is on the dog."

I basically had two leaving do's (parties). One was at a pub in one of the towns. The funniest thing that night was that my old boss and new boss, who never got along that well, and I was always in the middle, were having a grand old time together.

I wanted to treat every one of my mates in the Chase Pub one night. So I was able to have an invite only, and told them to run a tab for 200 pounds. That may not seem like a lot, but a pint was only about one and a half pounds. I think we went over, because they told me that was the largest single tab they ever had. But it was well worth it.

I was at the pub once, and someone was having a bachelor party, and I saw a blow-up sheep. "What's that?" I asked.

The answer came back. "A buggering sheep for the groom to enjoy."

All in all it was a once in a lifetime experience and very lucrative monetarily.

Bournemouth would have a super fourth of July party every year and it was a lot of fun being from the colonies! The British love sports and I was able to get the "Sports and Social" group to purchase some softball equipment and started a league.

Softball in the UK

Chapter 11

WINS 1996 - 2000

I arrived back in the States in November of 1996, and was pretty much a man without a home. I was to work in systems, but the new person in charge was originally from Manufacturers Hanover Trust and he had his own crew. I was reunited with my good friend, Lillian in NYC, who at least found me an office to use while I waited to see where I would wind up.

While I was waiting, I kept getting calls from Mr. M. from another systems area in the bank. He had heard about my success in the UK from another person in Securities Systems and wanted me to know if I would join him and take over the WINS system. I was really torn, because Ms. L. had made a large investment by sending me to the UK. On the other hand, I really didn't have a job. So, I called my old boss who had worked for her, and apprised her of the situation. She was great and asked what I wanted to do. I told her that I had a job, and I would rather be with someone who was chasing me than with someone who was ignoring me.

One funny thing happened at a party: The person that I was supposed to work for decided that he was going to test me. He didn't believe that I was so close with Chemical Bank senior management. At this party, the big boss from Payments Operations was standing behind me. I hadn't noticed, and my current boss said,

"Oh Bob, I think that you know Y. behind you?"

So I turned around and Y. saw me. He got a big smile on his face and said,

"Bob, great to see you again. What's going on? It's nice that you are back at the bank."

That cemented my decision. The only drawback was that I was going to be located back in Brooklyn. However, by this time there was a ferry service from NJ to lower Manhattan. It was expensive, but I would take it on Fridays and sometimes on Mondays. That made the trip a little better.

My new boss was just great and was shocked to see how low my salary was for a systems VP. He got me six figures within six months. As I was being introduced around, people were asking me what I ever did wrong to get the WINS system. I had no idea what a dog it was. Not to mention that the operations manager was a real pain.

Mr. M. was a great manager though, and he let me staff the team with my own people. As a result, I was able to bring my friend, Paula, over, and Ara, as a consultant. Plus, two really top notch systems people from Chemical who were being wasted in Treasury: Darren and Tammy. We had several not so hot consultants and slowly I moved them out. As it turned out, Tammy was good friends with one of my direct reports, so even better.

But back to the horrible system. It was part in-house and part external. The external system was the core, so to speak, and ran pretty well. That being said, it was a real task to conform to their updates. My first week on the job it crapped out just before 5 p.m. and the ops manager came up to torture everyone. He caught me going out the door and asked me where I was going. Now, I had to set the temperament and said, "Home." That wasn't the answer that he wanted and was fuming. I went on to tell him that my guys knew what was going on and they would handle the issue, which of course they did.

The next day, my guys were telling me that he was going to report me to my boss. I just laughed, as did Mr. M., after I explained my reasons. Another time, he came up after we had a systems update and was demanding that I fire the programmer responsible.

"I'm not going to fire someone every time a mistake is made. There would be no one left."

He kept bugging me, and finally I told him. "I made the change, so fire me."

I think he ratted me out again. I had to make it clear that we would get the system in shape and that he needed to give me time. It took a while, but he finally realized that things were improving, and he started to back off. We used to have weekly meetings. The first meeting after I promoted someone to a management position, the ops manager was picking him apart. After the meeting, my guy told me, "I wasn't expecting that."

I told him, "Remember in the Bugs Bunny cartoons where the wolf sees the sheep and they turn into lamb chops? You were the sheep today."

The worst thing about the system was that the batch ran for something like twelve hours, on a good day, so it was always late coming up in the morning. I had the team focus on that, and they found all kinds of useless things going on. For example, it was creating reports and files that were never used. This was chewing up cycles and CPU time, and costing a lot of money. My man, Darrin, got to work and eventually got the batch down to something like two hours. It saved $1,000,000 a year in CPU charges. Now this did not happen overnight, but the ops guy started to back off a bit once he started arriving for work and the system was up.

Another thing that was going on was that we had to run a monthly report for IBM that used so many boxes of paper, it would get delivered in a van! What a waste, and I can't imagine that anyone would read it. I came to find out that we were paying a consultant just to run this job every month because it would always crap out. That was all he did. Also, it was not a job that was in production, because the ops manager would not sign off. In essence, we should not have even been sending it to a client.

So first, I told the ops manager that I was not going to run it anymore until he agreed to put it into production. Well, he went nuts. Luckily, my boss backed me up. Then I told the guy's manager to cut him loose, and it went something like this:

"I can't. No one knows how it works."

"We have a month; someone will figure it out. He's holding us for ransom."

"Should I fire him today, or give him two weeks' notice?"

"It's up to you; you're the boss."

He decided to give him two weeks' notice and the guy was being a royal pain in the ass. After a few days, his manager came back.

"This guy's making me nuts. Can I tell him to leave now?"

"Yep, you should have in the first place."

"You knew this would happen, didn't you?"

"Yep."

"So why didn't you make me fire him right away?"

"You wouldn't have learned the lesson, correct?"

"No."

"So now you know, don't keep the dead wood hanging around anymore than you have to."

I got one of the top guys to look at it, and it was fixed and ready for production before the next run. I don't recall for certain, but I think we cut down the size also. That guy was gaming us by making out that it could not be fixed.

One thing that really pissed me off was that towards the end of one year, the Investment IT area was in a budget crunch and they were looking to save money. There was a big meeting and they asked for suggestions. I said that we could make all the consultants take two weeks off before the end of the year. We made the full-time staff take off two weeks, so why not do the same for the consultants? Bear in mind, they were generally paid more, and very rarely took time off. Well, a senior manager went ballistic and was saying it wouldn't work, and it did not make any sense.

A few weeks later we got the directive to do exactly what I proposed. That guy went to the top man and claimed it as his idea.

Over the course of four years, the team implemented so many improvements that we went from the worst system to the best system in our group. At one point, in 2000, I was approached by another team who asked if they could take Darren, who did so much to reduce our CPU charges, to look at their system. He identified over $5 million in savings for them. They were shocked when I agreed to let him go. I felt that saving $5 million was good for everyone and we were in great shape. We eventually got our batch down from twelve hours or more to about two hours.

Eventually, Mr. E. left and was replaced by a total incompetent. How this guy got hired is beyond me. At some point, someone got wind that he had drifted from job to job over the course of several years. Hard to believe that he would be selected for such an important senior position. Thankfully, he was gone in six months.

Our new boss was one of my peers, and while we were sort of friends, our philosophy on how to run a systems area was completely different. Especially when it came to coordinating the implementation of changes that were required when the vendor updated their system. My expert, KT, had it down to a science, and ever since she took over the coordination, we never had an issue. He wanted to add in layers of documentation that would just bog down the process, without adding any value. We had several battles over this, especially as I was just ignoring him. I wasn't about to rock the boat.

Everyone was in a panic over Y2K. But I had my friend, Paula, looking after it, and like almost everyone else, we did not have any issues. But everyone that I knew in systems and operations, were all up waiting for a system crash, rather than a ball drop.

Shortly after Y2K, the bank announced that they were moving Securities to Dallas, and Treasury to Tampa. I really liked my job by then, but I wasn't thrilled about Dallas. In hindsight, maybe that would have been the better choice, as my daughter now lives there. But at the time, I thought Tampa would be the better choice, as my brother lived in Florida. Also, my children were young, and I figured being near Disney World wouldn't be bad.

Once again, my friend, Lillian, stepped in and told me that she could get me back working for her boss, and we went from there.

Chapter 12

Tampa Move and Facilities
2000 - 2001

I had an interview with Lillian's boss, a really nice guy who was very happy to have me. But shortly after the interview, he called to apologize and told me that HR put pressure on him to hire an SVP who was without a job. He went on to explain that he knew that he would not stay, but that his hands were tied, and that he would find me a position as soon as he could. True to his word, he was able to get me over working for Lillian. A few weeks later, I was attending his retirement party. We had a new boss from outside the bank coming in to manage the move, and the group moving to Tampa.

I was to report to Lillian and she was to report to the new boss. There were a lot of rumors flying around about him, but of course, you never know fact from fiction. One of his first requests was for us to produce a monthly book with the financials, volumes of transactions and other pertinent information about each of the departments that reported to him. I think there were five. We didn't get any specific guidance, so we did the best we could gathering information from each department and putting the report together.

As a direct report, Lillian was to present the report at his staff meeting. As it turned out, she had to be somewhere that morning, so it was delegated to me. It didn't really phase me, even though I had never met the boss. I've been in these positions before. We worked until about 7 p.m. the night before, and the next morning I went over to Brooklyn. I handed him the report, and he told me to step outside. He began to tell me how awful it was, that there were no tabs, this is wrong, that's wrong. Needless to say, I was stunned.

I got back to Manhattan, and shortly after, Lillian came and asked, "How'd it go?"

I proceeded to tell her in animated style, not well at all. After a few tries, we figured out his style and what he was looking for, and things got better. I did have the dubious job of chasing his direct reports for the information and listening to them complain about gathering all this information every month. "Hey, I'm only the messenger."

He was an amazing numbers guy, and I swear he could open a report to the one error and tell you what was wrong. I could never understand how he did this.

I was put in charge of tracking the staff of anyone who was going to relocate to Tampa, who was going to get a stay bonus, arranging "look-see" tours, and eventually was his point person for Treasury Services regarding the construction of the three buildings in Tampa. So a lot of responsibility, and I was getting it from all sides.

One thing I learned very quickly was that he did not tolerate bullshit, which was fine, as I don't either, and that if you show fear, you're done. He expected and respected pushback, and people who were afraid didn't cut the mustard. It didn't take me too long to figure it out, although I did have second thoughts a few times.

Once we were traveling to Tampa together, and I told him I'd get the car and pick him up in Brooklyn at the entrance with the horseshoe driveway. I got there in plenty of time, and I was waiting and waiting, thinking that he was held up in a meeting. Finally, I saw him running around the corner.

"What are you doing here? You said to meet on the other side."

"No I didn't, I said at the horseshoe drive."

"No one meets here."

"Yes they do, you can't park around the corner."

It was a long flight.

After the first group moved to Tampa in late 2000, we set up his first town hall at the hotel across the way. Earlier in the day he was getting besieged by people and told me,

"People expect me to be in three places at the same time."

Later in the day, I was at the hotel and coordinating the hotel, audio visual stuff, dealing with a vendor, and other issues. Shortly after arriving, he came over to me and was grousing about his phone connection or something like that, and I said,

"You know you're not the only person that can't be in three places at the same time."

And as I walked away, I was thinking, *Oh crap, now I did it*. But, after the event he came over and asked,

"How did I do?"

"Great, it went very well."

"You're okay?"

"I'm fine."

"Okay, good."

So, you see my point about pushing back and being honest.

I can't remember exactly when it was, but he kept asking me if I was going to relocate to Tampa. I kept saying that I wasn't sure. He wanted to know what the problem was. I explained that in my old area and this area, people were getting stay bonuses, but because I left to come here, apparently, I was not eligible. So, he asked how much I wanted.

"I said, "Fifty thousand dollars."

"If I promise that you will get it, will you relocate?"

"Yes."

"I can't do it now, but I will get you that amount at year end. So you will relocate?"

"Yes."

At year end I had the amount I asked for and I called him up.

"I just wanted to say thank you."

"You didn't believe me, did you?"

"No."

"Let that be a lesson, when I say I am going to do something, I do it."

He did so many things for the staff that I don't think they really knew or appreciated. For example, the first holiday party. I recommended that he invite the spouses. He said that it was not the normal practice. I explained that it would be a nice gesture for the first group that had just left their families so close to the holidays. He replied, "You're right, do it." He also had big summer picnics on the campus and really cared about the staff and their families. He gave me a lot of leeway in ensuring that the staff moves were carried out in the best interests of the families.

The Dunk Tank

Eventually, Lillian was replaced by someone else. The big boss would often bypass her and call me directly when it came to the move. She wasn't happy, but I told her, "What am I supposed to do about it if he calls me and not you?" I told him one time, and he just laughed.

He was always open to suggestions. One day he was complaining about all the rental cars, and because people were arriving on the same plane, both would rent a car. I suggested that we could get a couple of pool cars and keep them at the sight. Then people could take a taxi to the campus and reserve the pool car. That worked out great and saved a lot of money. We were walking from the parking lot after testing out the pool car and he asked me a question. I don't exactly remember what it was, but when I gave the answer, he told me, "Thanks, I need you to tell me when I am being a pain in the ass."

"Err, it's not easy to tell your boss's boss that he's being a pain in the ass."

He laughed and said, "Pick your spots."

I did get to be known as his "right hand," especially when it came to the building construction. He wanted me to show him where his office was in building two after it was completed. They designated a dinky little office behind the cafeteria as his office. Now, his role was much more than just site manager, and I don't think they thought this out very well.

"Find something else."

A few weeks later I found the spot on the top floor that was originally meant to be leased. It was in the corner and had a nice view of Tampa. After much haggling, and making the case to his boss, I was able to plan a nice office, with an adjoining conference room and a board room. After it was all done, I noticed that they were placing a microwave oven right next to the board room.

"Don't put that there."

"It's in the plans. There is to be a microwave on either side of every floor."

"Well if you put it there, the first time someone heats their fish when a meeting is going on in the boardroom, expect a call to move it."

There was no microwave installed.

The day before the building opened, I had so much sway that people were coming over to me asking if everything was in the right spot. "Can we move anything around?" "Is the boss going to like everything?" It was really funny. I'm not going to say that I didn't relish the position.

I got pretty tight with the person who ran the cafeteria, as we both attended the NY Restaurant School. The boss didn't like fancy cakes and pies for group lunches, and I had to continually control the delivery. I would tell my buddy, "Another cream pie was delivered, you're killing me."

My family and I moved to Tampa in July of 2001, and into our home in November. We got a beautiful crystal vase from the boss when we moved in. Prior to that, on my fiftieth birthday, he had sent a big goodies tower. Not many bosses are that caring.

The incident that I think had the most impact on our relationship was when one of his direct reports claimed that he never confirmed he was going to relocate to Tampa. I got a call from the boss.

"Do you remember when we all went to the baseball game?"

"Yes."

"Do you remember why P. said he could not attend?"

"Yes, he said that he was house hunting."

"Did he ever tell you that he was not going to relocate?"

"No. In fact, I have him on the database as confirmed."

"Would you confirm this if asked?"

"Of course. It's true."

The boss was moving and he wanted all his direct reports there too. Which made perfect sense. This guy was pulling a fast one, apparently brokering some sort of settlement. Not fair.

My family and I moved to Tampa in July of 2001, and I was pretty much the boss's eyes and ears. This gave me a lot of power; more than I ever thought I would have. I did have a lot to say about the facility, as the boss would often let me do what I thought was best.

Then September 11th happened.

Chapter 13
The World Trade Center
1973 - 2001

View from the top July 1977

An interesting thing about the World Trade Center is that it was completed in May of 1973, the exact month and year that I began my banking career with Chemical Bank, and it was destroyed only a few months after I left NYC. It was really a special place in the heart of New Yorkers. Many of us traveled through there on the PATH or subway, or would catch a bus there, or just walk past it on the way to the office. Windows on the World was a great restaurant, and it was very eerie to be in an office with floor to ceiling windows, and to look down.

In 1993, my wife was working in 5 WTC for Dean Witter. I recall watching the TV from my office about a half mile away as people were coming out into the snow, and I kept calling my wife to see if she was okay. They had told people that they should stick around, so she went to the gym. All the while, I was thinking that she was caught up in the bombing. She worked there from 1981 until 1995, when she met me in England.

A bomb was put into a van and placed in the parking garage, with the hope that both towers would come down. Some believe that had the van been placed more strategically in the garage, the plot may have succeeded.

I was in my office in Tampa when the boss's secretary called me and told me to come to his office quickly, and that a plane hit the World Trade Center. His office had cable TV and they were speculating, like most, that a small private plane went off course, or got into trouble and hit the tower. As we were watching, the second plane hit, and we both turned and looked at each other. We were being attacked! The New Yorkers in Tampa very quickly understood the magnitude of the situation, as we knew the Trade Center's proximity to most of the financial institutions: the NY Stock Exchange and the Federal Reserve Bank. Then the reports came in about the Pentagon and the plane in Pennsylvania.

Chase US dollar payments were better from a processing standpoint from many other banks, as we had already moved some people there from NY, and so our team was split between two locations. Although the staff did not have as much experience, there were several senior managers there. We went into contingency mode very quickly.

One senior manager wanted to shut the site down completely, and only allow full-time Chase employees onto the site. I believed that we were pretty safe, and in actuality there wasn't any signage on the street that showed where we were located. I had to explain that we needed food services to come in, as there was no place near to eat. Also, that we needed the cleaning staff for the restrooms, and that almost all of the security staff were contracted by an outside firm. Finally, the boss in NY agreed, and that settled the debate. Our bank security person was ex-CIA and he confirmed my assessment.

One funny story was that someone received a fax that was written in Hebrew. Not being from NYC, that person mistook the Hebrew writing for Arabic, thinking it was some sort of threat. I took one look and knew. People from Florida were still worried, but I knew at least one Jewish person on the site and confirmed.

My wife and I both knew people from our old jobs who perished that day. Of the two people that I knew, one was a coworker from my Chase days in Brooklyn. The other was the husband of a coworker. Normally, I would not know the spouses of coworkers, but Shelley was an avid NY

Giants fan and I had season tickets, so he would sometimes buy a game off me. Once or twice, we even met and watched the game together. A great guy who wouldn't hurt a fly.

One coworker from ITEX also worked at Cantor Fitzgerald. The day before, his computer wasn't working and they told him not to hurry in on Tuesday as they would be checking it out. He got off the subway and saw one building on fire and figured, no work today, and went home.

My role in Tampa was mostly keeping the facility safe, getting food, and supporting the staff. This was all well and good, but I realized how much I missed the operations action. So when the boss came down, I asked him if he could find me a job back in operations.

A few days after 9/11, we experienced a tropical storm, and while it did not cause any major damage, most of us were not prepared for the impact.

My photo of the WTC July 1979

Chapter 14
Money Transfer Investigations
2001 - 2004

Luck would have it that there were two positions open at the time, due to the fact that some people were not going to move to Tampa. I was given the choice to work for my friend in Operations, or my friend from NY, in Investigations. I decided to work for my friend in Investigations, because I had never done it and figured it would be a challenge. Since we had been peers before and we both had a lot of respect for each other's knowledge and capabilities, it was an easy transition. Also, as they were using Pegasystems, something I built years before, I felt that I could catch on pretty quickly.

Shortly after I joined, my old boss from Chemical Bank also joined our area, in charge of Compensation. It was like old home week. I have to admit that our manager had his hands full with an ex-peer and an ex-manager to deal with, as all of us had our ego issues.

Honestly, I was a bit intimidated at first, as it had been some twelve years since I was in Money Transfer Operations, but after a while it started to come back. I started on the Domestic side and then switched over to the International. There was not much difference, other than the clients that we serviced.

The hardest part of the job was keeping the queue low, as we were dependent on so many outside forces. We had to rely on the timeliness of banks or departments that were out of our control. Not to mention, that the US banks were all recovering from the WTC attack.

I don't remember anything that was really a significant problem or issue, other than my friend and I would sometimes butt heads on how something should be done. I do remember one time when we agreed to let one relatively junior person present to him. I met with him before, and told him that she was very nervous, and to let her get through the presentation before asking any questions. He agreed. The meeting started, and not two minutes in, he started asking questions. So afterward, I went to see him. "I know, I know, I was supposed to wait."

By the time I got back into operations, the value and the dollar amounts had increased dramatically. Where at one time, a hundred million dollar payment was considered large, we were now processing payments that were well over one billion. I can just imagine today that the payments are probably hitting over a hundred billion.

There's not too much to say about these three years, as I quickly got back up to speed and it was great to be working with old friends from the New York days. One event that was taking place was that the bank realized that hurricanes and tropical storms could interrupt the processing. So we began to build a backup site in a warehouse near Orlando, roughly ninety miles from Tampa. The idea was that we could move staff there quickly and that the storm would not hit both places with the same impact. We now know that this is not the case.

Chapter 15
Client Access Call Center
2004 - 2006

In late summer 2004, I was asked to take over the department that handled calls from our top-tier global clients. We offered a system that I like to refer to as sort of a home banking for Fortune 500 companies. This allowed them to create payments in various currencies from a terminal in their office. While most of the clients were in the USA, it was an around-the-clock operation, and so my staff had to be ready to handle calls from home.

My new boss was Mr. V., a good guy that I had known for a few years. He also reported to Mr. I. that ran the site, so still all in the family. He was moving up and I was basically replacing him. I really liked the fact that very early on he told me that even though I was replacing him, it was now my department. Luckily, I inherited a very knowledgeable staff. However, there were a lot of challenges with the system itself, which did not make it easy for the staff.

The week I transitioned over from my old job, hurricane Charley hit Florida. The craziest thing was that for days the reports said it was going to be a direct hit on Tampa. We began to send staff to some safe places, even to NY and MA. My old department sent scores of people to Orlando for the first real test of the facility there. Early in the day they sent most of us who were still in Tampa home to work from there if the job permitted. I thought it was strange because the sun was shining and there was no wind. Just before leaving, the report came in stating that the storm made a forty-five degree right turn and was headed straight for Orlando. We wanted to stay, but were told no, and to go home. Just as I was pulling out, my old boss called and asked what was going on. I told him that the storm was headed straight for him in Orlando. He thought I was kidding. In the end, he and many others were stuck for days with no electricity, and because many roads were blocked, they could not just drive back to Tampa, for about a week.

On July 1, 2004, JPMorgan Chase merged with BankOne. There was no immediate impact, but as most mergers go, things started to percolate in 2005. More about that later.

Client Access had a lot of old legacy systems that were cobbled together from various mergers in the past. And as a result, if there was a problem, it could take some time to research and correct. One day, one of the systems took a really big hit and we were down for hours. The clients were extremely upset. For the major ones, we were able to devise some workarounds with our colleagues in Payments, but it was a disaster.

The next day, Mr. I. summoned myself and my boss to his office. Now, we were a dress down shop by then, and I showed up in a suit. Mr. I. said, "What's with the suit?"

"I figured if I'm going to a funeral, I might as well dress the part."

That wasn't the right answer. I think he got a lot of pressure from the top because he wouldn't let us explain how it was beyond our control. The next day, my boss was out of the office and I was summoned back. Mr. I. asked, "What was that all about yesterday?"

"What do you mean?"

"You didn't give me any answers."

"You wouldn't let me talk."

"Okay, you have thirty minutes, start talking."

To his credit, he let me explain and didn't interrupt. He asked what I thought could be done, and afterwards he realized that we could not control the system outage and do anything more than we did during the outage. I don't remember when it happened, but soon after he left and was replaced by a senior manager in Chicago from BankOne. Things started going downhill from there.

BankOne also had a Client Access system, but it was not nearly as robust and not global like ours. A real competition began for which system would survive. They claimed to have many more clients, which in a sense they did. However, most never made a payment.

Around mid 2006, Mr. I. left, and we were put under control of someone in Chicago. At first it seemed okay, but then the power play began. We had another big systems problem and this guy swore that he understood and that it had nothing to do with our service team. However, there was a lot of stuff going on behind the scenes. We had to take on someone who was supposedly an expert in customer service. But he did not understand our business and was trying to implement a retail philosophy that just would not work for our clients. He was also secretly reporting back nonsense to Chicago. By the end of the year, my boss was on the hook, and I think I was next. He was finally let go just before Christmas and I got a boss who also had no clue. That New Year's Eve, we had a big issue and she and the guy in Chicago were asking my advice, even though the writing was on the wall. I did make my feelings known, but got the job done.

Shortly after that I was moved out of my position and was a man without a job. I credit one of the inner circle people from my payments days at Chemical Bank for rescuing me. My new boss was a great guy, and they were proposing that I take some sort of training role. I had found out that there was a UAT manager role open, and explained that while I know nothing about training, I do know how to do UAT. Thankfully they agreed, and I began that role in 2007.

Chapter 16
Client Access Acceptance Testing
2007 – 2014

As I said earlier, I had a lot of experience from Chemical Bank doing User Acceptance Testing. The big difference was that I was testing for external clients, as opposed to internal bank operations. One advantage that I had this time around in UAT, was that because I spent twelve years as an IT manager, I could usually see through the underlying issues.

There was a team already in place from BankOne in Chicago. However, I also needed to start filling some positions in Tampa with staff that knew the JPMorgan system. At one of the first meetings, I listened in from Chicago, I heard one of my newly inherited staff members really take charge of a meeting. She became one of my best people. But I remember thinking to myself, this girl (I say girl, because she was about thirty years younger than me), is super. In any event, we really thought very much alike. Once I did a team building exercise, and one of the exercises had us put down our thought process. We were then sent to four corners: north, south, east, and west. K and I were the only northerners in the group. It was something we joked about for years, as we knew we were right about everything Even the southerners' "feelings" in business!

Check your traits:

- **North:** These individuals are focused on goals, goals, goals. They're <u>confident</u>, decisive, independent, and love to <u>check off a task</u>.

- **South:** Meet the team players of the group who check in with everybody's vision and feelings before getting started. Their inclusive approach is highlighted by superior patience and listening skills.

- **East:** These people thrive on well-laid plans. They approach their jobs with logic, organization, and a bird's-eye view. They consider the outcome of a project in its totality at the time of ideation.

- **West:** Like northerners, western employees take risks in the office. However, they're driven more by creativity, vision, and enthusiasm, rather than quick action. They strive for originality.

UAT had changed a lot over the years, and several tools were now available to write scripts, facilitate testing, track errors and so forth. It added a lot more structure than we had some twenty years earlier. Another thing that BankOne had that we did not have at JPMorgan Chase, were "Enterprise Releases" or ERs. These were scheduled six times a year, where all the business and IT teams would gather to ensure that all the tech implementations worked correctly, and that issues and customer impacts were logged and eventually corrected.

Shortly after taking over UAT, I was also given the role of ER manager for the Client Access business. This is where I had to focus most of my time. UAT was critical, but that was well under control by the staff in Chicago, so I did not need to worry about it. The ERs on the other hand, took a lot of planning, and there were projects that would move in and out. The reporting was horrendous.

At the beginning, there were six per year, and for some strange reason they would assemble all the IT and business people in Tampa. That made no sense to me. But I was able to make the case to send a small team from Tampa to Chicago where most of the IT people resided, rather than sending twenty or thirty people from Chicago to Tampa. I also made the three smaller releases virtual, so that most people could work in their office or from home.

I first encountered ERs when I was the Client Access manager. They would take over most of the conference rooms in Tampa. It is where I met two of my best friends at JPMorgan for the last five or six years, Steve and Lou. Lou was a natural, as he was a paisan from Brooklyn who was then working in Columbus Ohio. At that time, we were combining a lot of legacy systems, and at the end of the ER he came in with a box of

tee shirts that he made at his expense. There were two streams that were referred to as the big pipe and little pipe, and his shirts read:

"I laid the big fat pipe and loved it." The pipe was holding a flag that said "Va fangul."

We were taking bets as to when he would get his walking papers, but they never came. We got a lot of slack at the ERs as to what we could say. A lot of things would get you fired, but I think they let things ride because there was so much pressure put on everyone. And not only that, no one else was crazy enough to spend a week in confinement. In fact, we would have a board where we would write all the innuendos.

Now Steve was another trip. The first time I met him, all I would see him do all day was place red, amber, or green stickers on a board that showed the status of the ER issues.

I was thinking to myself, *they pay him for this?* Steve was one of the funniest guys I ever met. He was quite serious during business, but afterwards, a pisser. One time in Tampa, things went very well on a Saturday. So well, that Steve's boss told him to take the interns out for a good time. Apparently, a good time was had by all. So good, that everyone was late coming in on Sunday. When Steve arrived, his boss asked him, "Where is everyone?"

"I don't know."

"Didn't you take them out last night?"

"Yeah, but you didn't say anything about bringing them back."

I think she also asked him why he was late, and he said that he was at Mass.

By the time I took over, Steve was working as an employee in Lowell MA, and we would often be among the few that would get stuck very late at night. I wasn't one for wasting everyone's time and rather than keep a dozen or more people around, I would keep the most important. Steve and I were the best at torturing the IT guys to get the results we needed.

One night we were stuck, and the IT guys kept telling us it would be thirty more minutes. This was on a Wednesday, and typically we would be wrapping things up early and would head over to the Blue Martini for an ER ending celebration. We were there waiting to test, and it was about 6:30, and Steve said,

"Okay, it's six thirty. We'll do a quick test and be done at seven and be at the Blue Martini by seven fifteen."

Then we got the call that it would be another hour. Steve said,

"Okay, so at seven thirty we'll do a quick test, and be done at eight, and be at the Blue Martini by eight fifteen."

So this went on a few more times, and by the time we got done it was something like 11 o'clock and Steve said, "Let's go."

"Go where?"

"The Blue Martini. We can be there by eleven thirty."

"Steve, it's Wednesday, no one will be there."

"Sure they will. Come on, let's go."

We got there, and there was one person, the porter mopping up! Anyway, we did find an old man's bar somewhere in Chicago for the ER release celebration.

Another time, it was about midnight and Steve was formulating the end of day message to the bosses. He kept asking me about it, and I was telling him, "It's fine. Let's go already." This was going on for an hour, and finally I told him, no one was going to even open the mail, let alone read it. "They'll read it."

"Put a return receipt on it, you'll see." Two people read it.

For a while, we all had Blackberrys for phones and messages, and it was always a hassle to get a message to format correctly. So, there I was, waiting for Steve at Berghoff's for dinner and he was trying to get a message to look good. He kept sending, and asking, "How's it look now?" After a few times, I said "Good." It still looked like crap, but I was hungry. I told Steve to have them blame me.

Despite all the hard work, ERs were also a lot of fun, as we would always have a theme to keep things interesting. We would decorate the office and people were allowed to show up in some sort of dress or hat to go with the theme.

Every four months, one of my team of four would have to pull together conference rooms, phones, people, and food, all while keeping up with what was going into the release. It was no small task. Once the ER kicked off, there were five to six, twelve hour days, as we rolled through the implementation and necessary fixes to code. Not to mention, dealing with the business partners who could not grasp the complexity of it all.

I remember one particularly bad release, when the IT guys came up with plans A, B, C, D, and F. So naturally, one of us asked,

"What happened to plan E?"

"We don't have one."

That cracked us all up.

ER Photos

Chapter 17

The Eateries

In Manhattan and Brooklyn, both Chemical Bank and Chase had cafeterias, which for the most part were less expensive than eating on the street. When I started at Chemical Bank, they still had an officers' dining room, where the officers could go and have a really nice meal for very little money. I was invited there a few times as a non-officer and it was very nice. What stood out was the "Sundae Bar" where we could make our own sundaes. This little perk closed shortly before I became an officer. When I started at Chase, they still had the officers' dining room. If I remember correctly, they took out $60 a month, not a bad deal for restaurant quality food. I think it closed in 1990 or 1991.

Manhattan

Manhattan had so many great places to eat that it's hard to keep track and remember all the names. Some do stand out though.

Graziano's West - This was owned by my cousin, Mike, in the late 80's and early 90's. Super Italian restaurant. Very big and with a 40's look to it, with all wood paneling. At the time, I was attending the NY Restaurant School near 42nd St. in Manhattan and I used Graziano's for one of my papers.

The Italian Alps - This was a cafeteria style place that served pretty decent Italian food. It was very close and we were able to get our food quickly. We could then find a seat on any of the three floors in the building.

Fraunces Tavern - A colonial building located across the street and around the corner from 55 Water St. Very good food, in a colonial setting. Great breakfast and Bloody Marys. It has been there since 1762. In 1975, I walked past it about fifteen minutes before a bomb exploded.

Harry's at Hanover - The place to go for their Wednesday lunch special, Beef Wellington, with their sliced potato and creamed peas. Wash that down with a martini or two and you were set for the mid-week afternoon grind. I think it was about $15 in the late 80's, now $69 for dinner.

Wolfe's Deli was a great place for corned beef or pastrami sandwiches, knish, or a kosher hotdog.

Geradi's was a more upscale sit-down Italian restaurant with a bar. Very good food, especially the veal.

1001 Delights, I think that was the name, was good for a deli sandwich and a beer, and it was just across the street and down a few steps. They also had a few pinball machines.

There were two places that the names escape me. The first was a fast food pasta restaurant. You would select your pasta and sauce and they would cook it up quickly in about ten minutes. The other was an upscale white tablecloth place. They would give the menu with the prices to only the host, everyone else got a menu without prices.

Being Manhattan, there were a lot of pizza places and Chinese take out, one that stood out was Yips. And of course, we could walk to Little Italy and Chinatown. My favorite Chinatown place was Hau Yuan. They had mostly Chinese patrons and some great dishes, especially the eggplant in garlic sauce.

Of course, there were no shortages of bars, and we even had two inside the building at 55 Water St. On the lower level, there was a small bar called the Dinghy, and on the mezzanine level, there was a more upscale place with a restaurant called the Buttonwood.

Long before the food trucks, we had the ever present "dirty water hotdog" vendor. He and his wife were a staple for years out in front of 55 Water St., and they did some business.

I never went to the Chairman's dining room at Chase, but the Chemical Bank one was located at 20 Pine St on the top floor. It was decorated like an old southern mansion, and after lunch you were offered cognac and cigars.

Brooklyn

We had a very nice cafeteria in MetroTech, but there were not a lot of eateries on the street.

Junior's, famous for their excellent cheesecake, was also a great kosher deli, similar to Wolfe's in Manhattan, but much larger. I didn't eat there too often, but we were always ordering cheesecake from them for birthdays.

Gage and Tollner had been in business since 1879, and still had gas lamps in the place. It had American fare and was like going back in time almost one hundred years. I once met the former mayor of New York there, Ed Koch. They closed in 2004, and reopened in 2021, but no more gas lamps.

There was one really unique place, Kevin Barry's, that had entrances on two streets. If we went in one door, we were in an Irish Bar, and if we went into the other door, that had a different name over it, we were in an African-American place. But they were connected. I kid you not!

Bournemouth

As I stated earlier, we had the cafeteria/pub in the building. Back then, we also had a very nice coffee/espresso bar and the sports complex down the road. In Bournemouth itself there were several very nice restaurants.

Ocean Palace was an excellent Chinese restaurant, and I would try and have as many dinners there that I could. I highly recommend it if you are ever in the area.

I'm not a big fan of Indian food, but Eye of the Tiger was very nice. I'm not sure if they still provide the service, but when I was there you could have your food shipped to anywhere in the world. There was also a very nice Italian place, and of course, several great pubs.

One of my old friends from Chase in the UK, a Liverpool native, who was then still in America, came across to interview, to take my place. So, I took him to a pub in Bournemouth. If you are not familiar, you order your drink at the bar and place your food order. You take the drink with you, and they deliver the food. We were sitting there and finishing our first pint, and Dave said,

"Do you want another beer?"

"Sure."

"I'll get the waitress."

"She won't get the beer. She only brings the food."

He asked her for two beers. She looked at him like, the accent is right, but what planet are you from, and told him he had to order at the bar. I'm cracking up and Dave said, "Have I been away that long?"

"I guess so."

One of my favorite pubs was The Old Beams, in Dorset, not too far from where we lived in Ringwood. It dates to the 1600s and has a ceiling that is only about seven feet high. Great place to get the feel of an old country pub.

Singapore

I dined in several places in Singapore and can't remember the names of the places. But if you ever have the chance to go, you must try the Chili Crab and the Pepper Crab. There are so many great restaurants there that it's almost impossible to go wrong. In the heart of the Financial District there is a street food complex. Boat Quay is filled with great restaurants, and Clarke Quay houses bars and discos. Orchard Towers is an interesting place. By day, an office building, by night, four of the floors housed some of the more, shall we say, interesting bars and nightclubs. This part is known commonly as the "Four Floors of Whores."

During my first trip there, I stayed at the Hilton Hotel just across the street. The first night there, I went for a walk and a girl smiled at me, not thinking, I smiled back. The next thing I knew she was next to me asking me if I needed a date. I said "No, I'm good and I have jet lag. I'm just going back to the hotel to sleep."

"I'll make you sleep real good."

Thankfully by then I was in front of the hotel and was home free. The next day, I was telling my coworker from Singapore how friendly everyone was there and that someone wanted to date me.

"Don't you know what's there?"

"I do now."

Hong Kong

Like Singapore, Hong Kong is a Mecca for food. On my first trip in 1985, the Hilton Hotel had a buffet where you could order anything off of the menu for $20. I also had them take me to a Dim Sum restaurant for lunch. The servers would come around with trolleys filled with wicker baskets and you could select what you wanted, as everything was the same price. At the end, they would count the baskets and give you a bill. I stayed away from the chicken feet. I also took the team of twelve for a gourmet lunch, and it was a whopping $100. Those days are long gone. I did try the congee, but they wouldn't tell me what was floating around.

Chicago

Chicago is a great city for restaurants, and because I spent so much time there, I got to sample some really great places. My favorite Italian place was Rose Angelis, which unfortunately, has closed. It was north of Chicago and was in a house in a residential neighborhood. They also had garden seating in the summer. The first time we went there and we all ordered a meal, it was so much food that after that we would split everything two or even three ways.

The Italian Village was another great place and was on the walk home from the office to the hotel. They had three levels with a different menu on each level and was decorated old world style. It was a fun place with very good food. I also liked Quartino's a lot. They made small plates, so you can order a bunch and share. They also make great pizza. I highly recommend it if you are in Chicago.

Of course, there is the original Uno's deep-dish pizza, and Lou Malnati's deep dish and thin pizza. We would order this often for the ERs; always a good choice. Also, there are great sandwiches from Potbelly. And of course, there were other great places in Little Italy, Greek Town, and Chinatown. Don't forget to try an Italian beef sandwich.

Because we would typically be locked up for four to five days, I made it a point to have a pre-ER dinner on Friday nights. I would try to find a place with great food, and with a public atmosphere. There were also a couple of places where you could pour your own beer, wine, or spirits. You could set a limit and they would keep track of how much you poured. For German food, I liked Berghoff's. It had an old world setting and was very close to the Palmer House Hotel, where we would sometimes stay.

Miller's Pub, around the corner from the Palmer House, was also a good place for a quick inexpensive meal.

Across the river was the Shaw House, known for great seafood. I once ordered in dinner for the ER I think we went a bit over budget that time. For an interesting cheeseburger, the Billy Goat Tavern is a must! We loved to go to Fogo de Chao, for the Brazilian meat fest. It was one price for all you can eat. A bit expensive, but great if you want to chow down like a caveman.

The last few years that I went to Chicago, I tried to stay at the Wit hotel. It was a little bit further to walk to work from there, but it had recently been remodeled and had a really super rooftop bar, called the Top of the Wit. We spent many a night up there with a spectacular view of the loop area. One Sunday, we happened to get out early and planned to go to dinner. It was a nice summer day, and so a couple of us went up there to have a drink before leaving for dinner. When we arrived, there was an outrageous party going on, so we called everyone and said, "We're staying at the Wit." I think we spent the better part of everyone's per diem up there that day.

Speaking of per diem, we received $60 a day for breakfast and dinner. I would buy my breakfast, and the remainder worked out to be just enough to get two martinis and two small plates at Morton's bar. Not a bad deal. I loved the oatmeal at the Corner Bakery that was just across the street from work.

Mi Tiera, just outside of the city, was one of the best places to go prior to an ER release. An authentic Mexican restaurant, complete with a roving Mariachi band. They had a super birthday celebration, so we would always tell them that someone was celebrating. In another part of the restaurant they had a Mexican style disco, and it was beyond loud.

The Chase Cafe in Tampa

While not a five star restaurant, I mention it because it turned out to be the meeting ground of NY Payments people from Chase, Manny Hanny, and Chemical bank some forty years after we were all bankers in NYC. As the senior members of the staff, we could spend our lunch hours reminiscing about the days gone by.

The Greenery
(across the street from my apartment.)

If you're wondering why I would mention a restaurant across the street from my little apartment in Queens? For two reasons: First, it was a great place and my wife and I would go there on Friday nights when we were dating. Also, as a few of us in Payments Automation lived in Queens, sometimes we would eat there after a Saturday implementation.

But the most important reason is that it was the place where I witnessed my second shootout. It took place early in the morning after St. Patrick's Day, probably in 1983 or 1984. I woke up about 2:30 a.m. and heard a commotion in the street. I looked out the window and I saw a guy in the street getting kicked and stomped on. His friends were trying to distract a couple of guys and rescue him. He finally got up and started to run away. The three or four guys who were beating him were still standing there. I watched as the guy catching the beating went to his car and started to walk back. One of the guys started to walk back towards him and said, "I thought I told you to get the fuck outta here."

BAM! The guy grabbed a gun and was then chasing the other guy around a mailbox, firing wildly. At some point, he had him and could have blown him away. For some reason, he stopped and casually walked away.

I always suspected that the place was owned by someone in the mob, and I pretty much was convinced after what happened next.

A police car rolled up and the cops asked, "We got a call about a disturbance."

"Nothing happening here."

"Okay." And they drove away.

Nothing happening?! Like six shots were just fired off.

Right after that another car pulled up. Three guys in their late thirties or so went over to the guys who were in the altercation, who were in their mid-twenties, and started smacking them around.

The next day, I went to check the window of the restaurant and there were at least four bullet holes. It's amazing no one was killed inside or outside the place.

Chapter 18
Meeting the CEOs

Over the course of my forty plus years in banking, I met several of the CEOs. The first one that I met was Donald C. Platten. Mr. Platten was the CEO from 1973 to 1983. I met him as he toured our department and my boss's boss asked if I wanted to meet him. I said, "Sure, it's the least I can do."

And the boss told me, "That's what he said too."

Anyway, he was a very cordial man who shook everyone's hand and seemed very genuine. In those days, you went to a reception when you were promoted to officer.

I met Walter Shipley twice and heard him speak a few other times. When he came to our department, there was an entourage following him. I loved that when they tried to guide him, he would go in the opposite direction and walk into people's cubicles. He would ask them how they were doing, what their job was, and if they needed anything. He was very tall, six feet eight inches, so you could not miss him. Soon after his becoming CEO I heard him speak at a function, and he said that the best thing about being CEO was that you get to speak first. He recounted that as president of Chemical Bank, he had a speech with a catch phrase embedded in his remarks. As Mr. Platten finished his remarks, he announced, "From now on we will never say this phrase again."

Mr. Shipley said he then had to try and replace the phrase on the fly. One other notable thing about Mr. Shipley was that he was very clear that any take-over or bail-out of another institution was to be referred to as a merger. He felt this way because he said that NY Trust employees were not treated with respect when they were taken over.

It was some twenty years or so later before I met another CEO. By that time I was in Tampa, and the CEO, William B. Harrison, decided to hold the annual meeting in Tampa. I believe it was 2003. I was called in by the big boss in Tampa, still Mr. C., and was told that Executive offices contacted him to provide a key person who knew the site very well to act as an escort for a VIP. He wanted to know if I would be okay with being this escort. I was pretty honored to be asked, and of course, agreed.

I had no idea what to expect and was only told that I was to meet the treasurer of the Bank, Tom Horan, the day before, and he would tell me what was expected. At the meeting there were several people who had specific assignments, and Mr. Horan went through all the details. At the end, he asked for me specifically, and came over with another gentleman. He told me that both he and Mr. Harrison were grateful for my volunteering to usher the said VIP. He told me that the gentleman with him was the head of Chase security and that he would be with me the entire time. What they really needed from me was that if the VIP needed to make a phone call, needed a place to sit or use the restroom, that I would go with the security chief and her to the predetermined location. His parting words were, "I just want you to know that whatever she says or does is no reflection on you, and that Mr. Harrison and I appreciate what you are doing."

Whoa, hold on here. What's this all about? But before I could ask a question, they were gone with the wind. What I found out later was that she was a prominent gadfly who owned a small amount of shares in many major institutions, and she ran a sort of newsletter that raised questions about the companies she chose to focus on.

There I was the next morning waiting for the car to arrive, not knowing what to expect. There was no mistaking the woman who showed up in a mink coat, in Florida, in May, for my gadfly. The head of security was there with me and told me that he would guide her into the building. There was an x-ray machine set up at the entrance, and the security people asked her to remove her coat. After some protesting, she told the machine operator, "Be careful with that coat. It's worth more than you." Oh boy, here we go. Once she got through the machine and got her coat back, the security guy bolted, and I was left with her for the next three hours or so.

As there was some time before the meeting, she wanted to do things that I was told that she could not do, like tour the buildings for example. Finally, the board members started to arrive, and she went over and started breaking everyone's balls. I could not believe it. They all were pretty amenable to her nonsense, but probably smart to not get into a pissing contest.

Finally, the meeting started. She was mostly quiet, but I could see that she couldn't wait for the mic to open up, so she could start in. She was the first one up and started off by saying that Mr. Harrison was a good man, but his liars and flunkeys would not let her do this, or that, and the other thing. I had conscripted a buddy to help, and I think he went into shock at that point. I think she got up to the microphone a few times and would light into the officers and board members of her choosing.

After the meeting, I had to get rid of her, and I bolted to the phone to get her to her car. I couldn't get her out fast enough. Once everything was done, Messers, Harrison, and Horan thanked me again, and reassured me that they understood how difficult it was and not to worry.

The Sixty Second MBA

Not to knock anyone who took the time and spent the money to get an MBA, but a lot of it can be summed up in just some basic ideas, with a little street smarts sprinkled in.

1. Never lie to your boss. They will figure that out in the end. You don't want your staff lying to you.

2. Trust, but verify. Maybe a cliche, but you need to stay on top of the facts, lest you get burnt

3. Get rid of the dead wood quickly. They will only hinder your progress, even if someone tells you they are indispensable. Someone once asked me if it was hard to fire someone. "No, they fire themselves."

4. Don't ask your staff to do something that you would not do or have never done yourself.

5. Be fair. We all have favorites, but people understand that and will be fine with it, as long as everyone is treated fairly.

6. Don't bullshit people. You are usually not the smartest person in the room, so don't act like you are.

7. DON'T MICROMANAGE. This is in caps for a reason. Trust your staff.

8. Don't be afraid to make a mistake.

9. Be there with your staff when you have to be. Don't keep staff around when they are not needed. Send them home for some rest.

10. Most important of all: When things go well, give your staff the credit. When things go bad, take the heat.

The History of J.P. Morgan Chase

1799 - The Manhattan Company was founded.

1812 - The New York Manufacturing Company was founded.

1823 - The New York Chemical Manufacturing Company opened.

1839 - The Bank of Commerce opened.

1854 - Junius Morgan began in London.

1863 - First National Bank of Chicago opened.

1863 - Guaranty Trust Company NY began.

1868 - F.C. Sessions and Company opened in Columbus Ohio.

1868 - Drexel, Harjes & Company opened in Paris.

1871 - Drexel, Morgan & Company was founded.

1877 - Chase Bank opened in NYC.

1923 - Washington Mutual began School Savings Program.

1933 - National Bank of Detroit opened.

1955 - Chase Bank merged with The Manhattan Company.

1959 - J.P. Morgan merged with Guaranty Trust Company.

1961 - Manufactures Trust merged with The Hanover Bank.

1975 - Chemical Bank acquired Security National Bank.

1982 - Chemical Bank merged with Florida National Bank.

1987 - Chemical Bank merged with Texas Commerce Bank.

1989 - Chemical Bank acquired Horizon Bank NJ.

1991 - Chemical Bank merged with Manufacturers Hanover Trust.

1996 - Chase Bank and Chemical Bank merged.

1998 - Banc One merged with FNB Chicago.

2000 - J.P. Morgan merged with Chase Manhattan.

2004 - J.P. Morgan merged with Bank One.

2008 - J.P. Morgan Chase acquired Bear Stearns and Washington Mutual.

Stories from Friends

In 1995, Bob came to work in the UK at the Bournemouth payments processing location, and I was lucky enough to work in his team at that time. Bob brought a little bit of America with him, by first inviting us all to his house to watch the Super Bowl. We didn't understand much about the game, but we all had a great evening getting to know Bob a little better. We also enjoyed some of his excellent cooking. Bob also introduced us all to baseball. He got Chase to purchase all the equipment and he arranged interdepartmental games each week. I still have no idea what a 'fly ball' is, but it was great fun and a brilliant way to get to know people in other teams! Thanks Bob

-Ashley Smith, Bournemouth, UK

It wasn't easy for Bob coming to Chase Bournemouth to take over the IT Funds Transfer Team. In those days, it was still developing in house payments and cash management applications, alongside being responsible for the support and maintenance of the core Payments System, and the Nostro Reconciliation System. It was still a very technical and very competent I.T. team.

He appeared brash, confident, and loud initially, a typical New Yorker in my eyes. But once myself and the team got to know him, we all found him to be a great listener, fast learner, big supporter of the team and the individuals within it, and with a great sense of humour. He quickly became a part of the team and someone we could trust.

I always remember Marian, his wife, saying to me that she now knows the origins of Bob's humour, by being in the U.K. She was amazed that we found him funny and actually laughed at his jokes!!

Bob always did what he said he would do. With the politics at Chase, especially between New York and Bournemouth, that meant doing the right thing for the Bank, which was never easy. But his integrity and honesty cut through most of the bullshit that was prevalent at the time. To this day, Bob continues to challenge himself, and always does what he sets out to do. And I am sure, still cuts through any and all bullshit that he encounters.

Bob and I have remained friends ever since he came over to Bournemouth all those years ago.

- Jonathon Ashton, Bournemouth, UK

I used to call you Mr Zippy, because you just zipped around so fast. I've got some good night shift stories about when you were my VP and I was the officer in charge of Asia Night Shift. That one guy, and I'm sure you remember what he did. I handled it that night. I will not say anything more here. I would add to Elaine's comment, that the gentleman mentioned was a master at his craft and had things well in hand.

-Elaine Tengelsen, Tampa, FL

There I was. Green as a cucumber, reporting to Bob Sorrentino. I was responsible for all of the production on a mainframe accounting system. Our business owners/partners were probably the toughest and most demanding of any technical organization. When they walked on the floor, you could hear the hush until they moved on. There's nothing like fear and intimidation to run a tight ship. I can count how many times I sensed someone standing behind me first thing in the morning, just waiting for me to notice him, so he could ream me for whatever happened during the night. That was Mr. A.

So to establish better relations, Bob decided he would host a meeting every Friday afternoon with Mr A., Miss I., and several other high ranking VPs, to discuss what went wrong, what I was doing about it, and what was coming up over the weekend. It was me and them. Bob would sit back and watch, taking copious notes. Do you remember the cartoons when the wolf would spot his prey, and he would imagine them to be a roasted lamb? I was the lamb. Every Friday they tortured me and devoured me in their minds. This amused Bob. He would egg them on, while he took copious notes. I don't know what he did with those notes, but at the time I had a special place for them. If only he knew.

- Jim Rizzuto, Dallas, TX

I was very excited knowing I was going to report to you....that excitement was short lived. I did want to learn the business in depth. Gene M. was my mentor but was being moved to investigations. I was very upset about you leaving, I knew it was not going to be easy for me......things worked out in the long run. But I knew you did the right thing for yourself. I believe you moved to London, which was an incredible opportunity. I wished you would have taken me with you...

-Bill Serrapica, Tampa, FL

I was privileged to get to know Bob in the early nineties...working for a US company in the UK. It was only a matter of time before being exposed to the archetypal 'loud American' we'd all heard about, but never really experienced. There was nothing to fear, however, as Bob's congenial personality and management style was like a breath of fresh air. I have very fond memories of the pride he had in his Italian/American heritage. Also for the wonders he worked, in terms of inculcating a true sense of team and camaraderie across the broader payments technology organization he headed up in our European HQ. I vividly recall his energy and leadership qualities that inspired a few dozen of us Brits to participate in a highly competitive and enjoyable after work league dedicated to 'softball'...a very close cousin to baseball. Halcyon days.

-Andrew Savva, Bournemouth, UK

Upon first meeting Bob, he gave the impression of a serious, no-nonsense person. Eventually I realized that yes, while Bob is the consummate professional, he is very earnest when it comes to his kindness and consideration of colleagues and friends. Bob is far from superficial as he revealed himself to be a warm, funny, and friendly person. Not only that, Bob can read people to the point that he believes in them enough to allow them to prove their value, to not only others, but to themselves. Bob will always be one of the wisest and coolest people that I have known. They don't make 'em like Bob anymore!

Bob, thank you for your guidance, mentorship, and friendship.

-Jorge Diaz, NYC

How do you rebuild a web application used by 25,000 global clients to move billions of dollars every day? You start by hiring the best.

The organizational challenges seemed insur-mountable. Legacy platforms were effective, but the competition constructed a better mousetrap. By focusing on experience, they were winning over clients, and challenging one of the firm's primary revenue streams. A large program to build a competitive offering was underway, but it was over budget and behind schedule. Management pressure, demanding requirements, new technologies, and complex development made testing particularly challenging. The program was struggling and falling behind schedule.

Solution? Hire Bob. With years of product, technology, and operational experience, Bob was the right person for the job. He demonstrated leadership, patience, and skill in setting up the testing structure, developing the test plan, and managing the testing process. His attention to detail, coupled with his ability to collaborate with other program teams, stabilized the development process, and ultimately ensured a new app with an award winning client experience was rolled out to the highest possible standards and rave reviews.

-Iggy Khan, Chicago

Bob was a pleasure to work with on the global payments initiative for Chase in the mid-1990s, how the bank should rethink the cash management infrastructure for the future of banking. He was solid in thinking, and as important, shared a great sense of humor.

-Randy Schaffer, NY, NY

"From the time Bob joined Chase 30 or so years ago, I saw that he was different from all other managers. He treated his staff well, they were very dedicated to him, and most importantly, he got things done as painlessly as possible. I learned how to manage from him.

We have been friends since, as have our families. We talk of the old days and the new events. But he still can tell the old stories like they happened yesterday, and entertain, as he does with this book."

-Ara Jamgochian NYC

About the Author

Robert was born in Whitestone NY and grew up in College Point. During his childhood he spent a great deal of time at his maternal grandmother's house in Corona. Both of his parents' families had strong Italian roots and followed traditions from Italy. After retiring from banking in 2014, he began to dedicate his time to finding his roots in earnest. In 2018 he started a blog, and the following year a podcast, both to promote the research of Italian ancestry. In October of 2022 he published his first book, "Farmers and Nobles" the story of his two Italian-American families and how their lives in America were very similar, although centuries ago the families came from two very different socio-economic classes in Italy.

© Italian Market Place LLC

Also by Robert Sorrentino

Farmers and Nobles - Book

Italian Roots and Genealogy – Podcast and Blog
https://italianrootsandgenealogy.buzzsprout.com

www.ingramcontent.com/pod-product-compliance
Lightning Source LLC
Chambersburg PA
CBHW051944160426
43198CB00013B/2299